About this book

Symbols are used to denote the following categories:

✚ map reference
✉ address or location
☎ telephone number
◷ opening times
✋ admission charge
🍴 restaurant or café on premises or nearby
Ⓤ nearest underground train station

🚌 nearest bus/tram route
🚆 nearest overground train station
⛴ nearest ferry stop
✈ nearest airport
❓ other practical information
ℹ tourist information office
▶ indicates the page where you will find a fuller description

This book is divided into five sections.

Contents

Planning

Before you go

WHEN TO GO

JAN	FEB	MAR	APR	MAY	JUN	JUL	AUG	SEP	OCT	NOV	DEC
6°C	7°C	10°C	13°C	17°C	20°C	22°C	22°C	19°C	14°C	10°C	7°C
43°F	45°F	50°F	55°F	63°F	68°F	72°F	72°F	66°F	57°F	50°F	45°F

🔵 High season 🔵 Low season

London experiences defined seasons. Spring (March to May) has a mixture of sunshine and showers although winter can drag on into March. Summer (June to August) can be unpredictable; clear skies and long hot days one day followed by humid and overcast conditions the next. June has the advantage of long daylight hours; July and August are the hottest and the busiest with long school holidays. September is the official start of autumn, but often retains a summery feel, with October the real start of the season and the colder days setting in during November. Winter (December to February) is generally fairly mild, often wet and windy, any snow or very cold conditions not lasting long. The tip is to be prepared for any eventuality, dress in layers and take an umbrella. For a five-day weather forecast: www.bbc.co.uk/weather

WHAT YOU NEED

● Required   Some countries require a passport to
○ Suggested   remain valid for a minimum period (usually
▲ Not required   at least six months) beyond the date of
entry – check before you travel.

	UK	Germany	USA	Netherlands	Spain
Passport (or National Identity Card where applicable)	▲	●	●	●	●
Visa (regulations can change – check before you travel)	▲	▲	▲	▲	▲
Onward or Return Ticket	▲	○	○	○	○
Health Inoculations (tetanus and polio)	▲	▲	▲	▲	▲
Health Documentation (► 9, Health Insurance)	▲	●	●	●	●
Travel Insurance	○	○	○	○	○
Driving Licence (national)	●	●	●	●	●
Car Insurance Certificate	▲	●	●	●	●
Car Registration Document	▲	●	●	●	●

WEBSITES

www.visitlondon.com
www.londontown.com
www.visitbritain.com
www.enjoyengland.com
www.ba.com
www.nationalrail.co.uk

TOURIST OFFICES AT HOME

In the USA

7th floor, Suite 701,
551 Fifth Avenue,
New York, NY 10176,
☎ 1-800/462-2748
www.visitbritain.com

In Australia

Visit Britain
Level 2, 15 Blue Street
North Sydney, NSW 2060
☎ (02) 9021 4400 or 1300 85
85 89

HEALTH INSURANCE

Citizens of the EU and certain other countries receive free or reduced-cost emergency medical treatment in Britain with the relevant documentation (EHIC or European Health Insurance Card), but private medical insurance is still advised, and is essential for all other visitors.

Emergency dental treatment may be available free of charge if you can find a National Health dentist willing to treat you. A list can be found in the Yellow Pages. Dental treatment should be covered by private medical insurance.

TIME DIFFERENCES

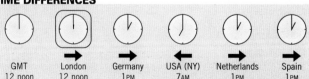

GMT	London	Germany	USA (NY)	Netherlands	Spain
12 noon	12 noon	1PM	7AM	1PM	1PM

London is on Greenwich Mean Time (GMT) in winter, but from late March until late October British Summer Time (BST, ie GMT+1) operates.

NATIONAL HOLIDAYS

1 Jan *New Year's Day*

Mar/Apr *Good Friday, Easter Monday*

First Mon May *May Day Bank Holiday*

Last Mon May *Spring Bank Holiday*

Last Mon in August *August Bank Holiday*

25 Dec *Christmas Day*

26 Dec *Boxing Day*

Almost all attractions close on Christmas Day. On other holidays some attractions open, often with reduced hours. There are no general rules regarding the opening times of restaurants and shops, so check before making a special journey.

WHAT'S ON WHEN

January/February

Lord Mayor's Parade (1 January): this procession of floats, bands and classic cars (from Westminster Bridge to Berkeley Square) attracts around a million onlookers.

Chinese New Year (late January–early February): human dragons and firecrackers light up Soho's Chinatown.

March/April

(University) Boat Race (late March–early April): Oxford against Cambridge over 6km (3.5 miles) of the Thames from Putney to Mortlake.

Battersea Easter Show (Easter Sunday and Monday): central London's best funfair with an Easter Parade on Sunday afternoon.

London Marathon (third week in April): some 30,000 runners, from world-class athletes to fancy-dressed 'fun-runners', pound the streets from Blackheath (Greenwich) to the Mall.

May

May Fayre and Puppet Festival (Sunday closest to 9 May): an annual celebration of England's first recorded Punch and Judy Show, staged in Covent Garden in 1662.

Chelsea Flower Show (late May): the world's best horticultural show, held in the grounds of the Royal Hospital.

June/July

Trooping the Colour (second Saturday in June): an inspection and parade of the guards honours the Sovereign's official birthday (apply for tickets well in advance).

Wimbledon Tennis Championship (last week June, first week July): you can line up for early rounds but it's advance ticket-holders for the latter stages.

Henry Wood Promenade Concerts (mid-July to mid-September): Britain's best-loved concert series occupies the Royal Albert Hall for three months.

August

Notting Hill Carnival (August bank holiday weekend): Rio comes to London with the biggest street festival in Europe.

September

Festival of Street Theatre (second and third week): a great time to be in Covent Garden.

Thames Festival: a celebration on the South Bank of the river, culminating in spectacular fireworks.

October–December

State Opening of Parliament (late October to early November): pomp and ceremony as the Queen arrives at Parliament in the Gold Coach.

London-to-Brighton Veteran Car Run (first Sunday in November): a great spectacle as Hyde Park is crammed with Chitty Chitty Bang Bang lookalikes.

Lord Mayor's Show (second Saturday in November): London's best traditional street parade, from Mansion House to the Royal Courts of Justice.

Christmas Lights (mid-November to early January): Regent Street and Oxford Street glow with the latest festive creations.

Getting there

BY AIR

London Heathrow Airport

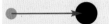

25km (15.5 miles) to city centre

🚆 15 minutes

🚌 40 minutes

🚗 40 minutes

London Gatwick Airport

48km (30 miles) to city centre

🚆 30 minutes

🚌 70–90 minutes

🚗 60–75 minutes

There are direct flights to London from all over the world. London has two main airports, Heathrow and Gatwick, with smaller airports at Luton, Stansted and London City (Docklands). There are train links to Paris and Brussels, and good road links to the Channel ports.

BY TRAIN

Visitors from Europe can come by train through the Channel Tunnel. Foot passengers can use the Eurostar trains (☎ 08705 186186; www.eurostar.com), which offer a direct link between Paris or Brussels and London (St Pancras International) in under three hours. The car-carrying train Eurotunnel (☎ 08705 35 35 35; www.eurotunnel.com) operates between Calais in France and Folkestone in England and takes around 35 minutes.

OTHER OPTIONS

Passenger and car ferries operate from Ireland, France, Belgium, the Netherlands, Germany, Scandinavia and Spain (www.ferries.co.uk). Trains link the arrival ports directly with London.

Long-distance coaches generally arrive at Victoria Coach Station close to London Victoria main line and underground rail station (☎ 08075 80 80 80; www.nationalexpress.com).

Getting around

PUBLIC TRANSPORT

Internal flights Internal flights link Northern Ireland, Scotland, Wales and the regions with many of London's airports. London City Airport is in Docklands, less than 10km (6 miles) from the City financial district.

Trains London is at the centre of Britain's rail network, with lines going out from its principal stations – north from King's Cross, northwest from Euston, east from Liverpool Street, west from Paddington, southwest from Waterloo, south from Victoria and southeast from Charing Cross. A comprehensive suburban rail network complements the underground.

Buses London's red double-decker buses cover the capital in a network of services. A red bus stop symbol on a white background indicates that the bus must stop (unless it is full); at a white symbol on a red background you must hail the bus by putting out an arm. On some buses you must buy a ticket before boarding – available from machines at the bus stop, newsagents or tube stations. Travel cards are more cost effective.

River transport There are regular services from Westminster to the Tower of London, Greenwich and Docklands. Sightseeing boats are frequent and popular, and offer some of London's most memorable views.

Underground The underground, or tube, is the quickest way to get around London. Maps are on display at stations, on platforms and on the trains, and lines are named and colour-coded. Tube trains run from around 5:30am to around midnight.

TAXIS

London's famous licensed black cabs (which confusingly also come in various other colours) are very reliable with specially trained drivers. Hail them in the street when the yellow 'For Hire' sign on the roof is lit.

DRIVING

- The English drive on the left side of the road.
- Seat belts must be worn in front seats at all times and in rear seats where fitted.
- Random breath tests may be carried out, especially late at night. The limit is 35 micrograms of alcohol in 100ml of breath (Blood Alcohol Content .05%). Never drive under the influence of alcohol.
- Fuel is sold in litres and is available as unleaded, lead replacement petrol (LRP) or diesel. In central London, fuel stations are few and far between but there are many open 24 hours on the main roads leading away from the centre and in the suburbs.
- Speed limits are as follows:
  On motorways and dual carriageways: 112kph (70mph)
  On main roads: 80–100kph (50–60mph)
  On minor roads: 50–65kph (30–40mph)

TRAFFIC CONGESTION

The average vehicle speed in London today is 16kph (10mph), not much faster than it was in 1900! Some 5 million people per day choose to ride on the bus and tube network. Congestion charges in the 'inner ring' of the city (£8 per day; exemptions for disabled and alternative fuel vehicles) are now in force on weekdays (7am–6:30pm) to ease the traffic problems.

CAR RENTAL

The leading international car rental companies have offices at all London airports and you can reserve a car in advance. Local companies offer competitive rates and will deliver a car to the airport .

FARES AND CONCESSIONS

Students and senior citizens Holders of an International Student Identity Card and senior citizens can obtain some discounts on travel and entrance fees. There are a few good youth hostels in London (www.yha.org.uk).

The London Pass This is a pass to over 55 top attractions as well as an option for travel on buses, tubes and trains. The aim of the pass is to fast track and save money at selected major attractions. The pass is valid for either one, two, three or six days. It also offers discounts on restaurants and leisure activities. For further information www.londonpass.com

Being there

TOURIST OFFICES
London Tourist Board Tourist
Offices:

Main office
Britain and London Visitor Centre,
1 Lower Regent Street
☎ 0870 156 6366

Other offices
City of London
St Paul's Churchyard
☎ 020 7332 1456

Southwark
Vinopolis, 1 Bank End
☎ 020 7357 9168

Richmond
Old Town Hall, Whittaker Avenue
☎ 020 8940 9125

Twickenham
The Atrium, Civic Centre,
York Street
☎ 020 8891 7272

MONEY
Britain's currency is the pound sterling (£), issued in notes of £5, £10, £20
and £50. There are 100 pennies or pence (p) to each pound and coins
come in denominations of 1p, 2p, 5p, 10p, 20p, 50p, £1 and £2. Travellers'
cheques may be accepted by some hotels, shops and restaurants.
Travellers' cheques in pounds are the most convenient. Exchange offices
are common in central London, but they often offer poorer rates of
exchange. Credit and debit cards are widely accepted.

TIPS/GRATUITIES

Yes ✓   No ✗

Restaurants (if service not included)	✓	10%
Tour Guides	✓	£1–£2
Cafés/bars	✗	
Taxis	✓	10%
Chambermaids	✓	50p–£1 per day
Porters	✓	50p–£1

POSTAL SERVICES

Post offices are open Mon–Fri 9–5:30, Sat 9–12. The exception is Trafalgar Square Post Office, 24–28 William IV Street, open Mon–Fri 8:30–6:30 (Tue from 9:15am), Sat 9–5:30.

TELEPHONES

The traditional red phone boxes are now rare; instead, kiosks come in a wide variety of different designs and colours, depending on which phone company is operating them.

Coin-operated telephones take 10p, 20p, 50p and £1 coins, but card-operated phones are often more convenient. Phonecards are available from many shops. Hotel phones are very expensive. To call the operator dial 100.

International dialling codes
From London to:
Germany: 00 49
USA: 00 1
Canada: 00 1
Netherlands: 00 31
Spain: 00 34

Emergency telephone numbers
Police: 999
Fire: 999
Ambulance: 999

You can also dial 112

EMBASSIES AND CONSULATES

Germany ☎ 020 7824 1300
USA ☎ 020 7499 9000

Netherlands ☎ 020 7590 3200
Spain ☎ 020 7235 5555

HEALTH ADVICE

Weather Although London is not renowned for its sunny weather, the sun can shine a lot in July and August, when many Londoners take to the parks to sunbathe. Some sights involve being outdoors for prolonged periods: 'cover up', apply sunscreen and drink plenty of water.

Drugs Prescription and non-prescription drugs and medicines are available from chemists/ pharmacies. Pharmacists can advise on medication for common ailments. Pharmacies operate on a rotating basis so there is always one open; notices in all pharmacy windows give details.

Safe water Tap water is safe to drink. Mineral water is widely available but is often expensive, particularly in restaurants.

PERSONAL SAFETY

London is generally a safe city and police officers are often seen on the beat (walking the streets) in the central areas. They are usually friendly and very approachable.

To help prevent crime:

- Do not carry more cash than you need
- Beware of pickpockets in markets, on the underground, in tourist sights or crowded places
- Avoid walking alone in dark alleys at night

ELECTRICITY

The power supply in Britain is 240 volts.

Sockets only accept three (square)-pin plugs, so an adaptor is needed for Continental and US appliances. A transformer is needed for appliances operating on 110–120 volts.

OPENING HOURS

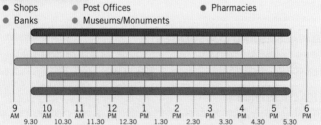

The times shown are traditional opening hours. Many shops in the West End open for longer hours and also on Sunday. High Street banks are open Saturday morning and exchange offices are open daily until late. Smaller museums may close one day a week. When pharmacies are closed a sign in the window gives details of the nearest one that is on 24-hour duty.

LANGUAGE

The most famous aspect of the Cockney language is rhyming slang, an insiders' vocabulary which was developed among street traders for clandestine communication. For example telephone becomes 'dog and bone', and may be abbreviated just to 'dog'! Below are a few examples. You may hear the occasional word in a locals' pub or shouted out at street markets. In the latter case it may well be tongue-in-cheek, a touch of local colour put on specially for British tourists as much as foreign visitors. If you want to delve more deeply, you will find whole books and even mini-dictionaries devoted to the language of Cockney rhyming slang.

Common Cockney rhyming slang

apples and pears *stairs*
barnet (fair) *hair*
boat (race) *face*
daisy roots *boots*
dog and bone *telephone*
(h)'alf inch *pinch, steal*
'ampstead 'eef *teeth*
have a butcher's (hook) *to have a look*
jam jar *car*
loaf (of bread) *head*
mince pies *eyes*
my old china (plate) *mate, friend*
plates (of meat) *feet*
porky (pie) *lie*
rabbit (and pork) *talk, chatter – usually meaningless*
rubadubdub *public house*
tea leaf *thief*
tit fer (tat) *hat*
trouble (and strife)/Duchess (of Fife) *wife*
two an' eight *state/mood*
whistle (and flute) *suit*

Other common colloquialisms to be heard in London

Awright mate? *How are you?*
boozer *pub (or person who drinks heavily)*
bobby, copper, the (old) Bill *policeman*
bovver *trouble, fighting*
chippy *fish and chip shop*
a face *a well-known person*
geezer *man, person*
guv *boss*
fag *cigarette*
innit *isn't it (at end of sentence and not meant as a question)*
leave it out! *stop it*
scarper *to run away*
the smoke *London*
the sticks *the provinces (anywhere outside London)*
straight up *honest*
sussed out *found out*
wotcher mate *another familiar term of greeting*
would you adam and eve it? *Would you believe it?*

Best places to see

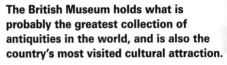

1 British Museum

www.british-museum.ac.uk

The British Museum holds what is probably the greatest collection of antiquities in the world, and is also the country's most visited cultural attraction.

Founded in 1753 from the collection of Sir Hans Sloane, the BM (as it is known to its regulars) has occupied its present site since 1823. The world's oldest museum has 4km (2.5 miles) of galleries displaying objects representing almost every aspect of international cultural history. The £100 million Great Court, designed by Sir Norman Foster and opened to the public in December 2000, is Europe's largest covered square.

The following are just a few of the BM's greatest and most popular treasures. Pick up a floor plan to locate them: Starting on the ground floor, the sculptures from the Parthenon (the Elgin Marbles) are widely held to be the greatest works of their kind from ancient Greece. The adjacent Nereid Monument, from Xanthos, Turkey, is a striking reconstructed temple. For more breathtaking sculptures on a monumental scale see the Assyrian human-headed winged bulls of Khorsabad. The museum has the greatest collection of Egyptology outside Cairo, including the famous Rosetta Stone, which enabled scholars to decipher the meaning of hieroglyphics. Not so renowned but equally worthwhile are the Oriental Collection (particularly the Indian sculptures) and the Mexican Gallery, both of which contain outstandingly beautiful works of art.

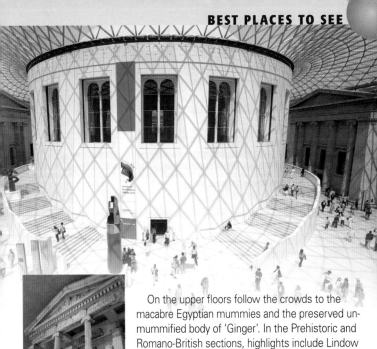

On the upper floors follow the crowds to the macabre Egyptian mummies and the preserved un-mummified body of 'Ginger'. In the Prehistoric and Romano-British sections, highlights include Lindow Man, the Sutton Hoo Treasure, the Mildenhall Treasure and the Lewis Chessmen. The Clocks and Watches collection is one of the finest in the world. Be there on the hour when the clocks chime in unison. Easily overlooked among the antiquities from Greece and Rome is the Portland Vase, a priceless example of the art of glass-making.

✚ 131 C6 ✉ Great Russell Street, Bloomsbury ☎ 020 7323 8000 🕐 Main museum Sat–Wed 10–5:30, Thu, Fri 10–8:30; Great Court Mon–Wed, Sun 9–6, Thu–Sat 9am–11pm. Reading Room: daily 10–5:30. Closed 24–26 Dec, 1 Jan, Good Fri 💷 Free 🍴 Café (£), restaurant (££) Ⓣ Holborn, Tottenham Court Road, Russell Square 🚌 New Oxford Street 7, 8, 19, 22b, 25, 38, 55, 98; Tottenham Court Road northbound and Gower Street southbound 10, 24, 29, 73, 134; Southampton Row 68, 91, 188

2 Covent Garden Piazza

www.coventgardenmarket.co.uk

London's most continental square is thronged with shoppers and sightseers by day, and with theatregoers and revellers by night.

Covent Garden Piazza was laid out in the Italian style in 1630 by Inigo Jones. Initially it was a very fashionable address, but from 1670 onwards, with the advent of the main London fruit, flower and vegetable market, it deteriorated and developed into a notorious red-light area. In 1830 its handsome centrepiece iron and glass hall was erected and the market continued trading at Covent Garden until 1974, when, finally defeated by transport logistics, it moved south of the river to Vauxhall. The site was then developed as a pedestrianized area, accommodating dozens of small shops and restaurants. The fruit and

vegetable stalls were replaced with the Apple Market, home to crafts, jewellery, clothing, accessories and antiques and collectables.

Today, only some arcading and St Paul's Church remain of the original Piazza. By the church portico street performers (licensed by the Covent Garden authorities) entertain large crowds daily. It was here, in 1662, that England's first ever Punch and Judy show was staged. St Paul's is known as the Actors' Church because of the large number of commemorative memorials (and graves) of screen and stage stars it holds. It is well worth a look inside and its garden is a remarkably peaceful oasis amid the general hubbub.

Major attractions around the Piazza are the London's Transport Museum, the Cartoon Museum and the splendid Royal Opera House.

✠ 131 E7 🚇 Covent Garden

3 Houses of Parliament (Palace of Westminster)

www.parliament.uk

The home of the Mother of Parliaments, and a masterpiece of Victorian Gothic, has over 1,000 rooms and the world's most famous clock tower.

The Houses of Parliament, seat of British government, date back to c1050, when William the Conqueror built his Palace of Westminster on this site. It evolved into a parliament around the mid-13th century and continued to be used as a royal palace until 1512, when Henry VIII moved his court to Whitehall. In 1834 a disastrous fire burned everything above ground (with the exception of

Westminster Hall, the cloisters and the Jewel Tower), and so construction began of the building that you see today. The principal architect was Charles Barry, though the flamboyant Gothic decorative touches are the work of his assistant, Augustus Pugin. By 1860, some 20 years later than planned and around £1.4 million over budget, it was virtually complete. The best-known part of the Houses is the clock tower, referred to as Big Ben – though to be precise this is the name of the great 13-ton bell that chimes every hour. After dark a light above the clock face indicates when Parliament is 'sitting' (when it is in session).

The modern Houses of Parliament divide principally into two debating chambers. The House of Commons consists of Members of Parliament (MPs), the elected representatives of the British people. Their functions are legislation and (as opposition) government scrutiny. The House of Lords is a body of unelected peers who examine proposed legislation from the Commons and also act as the highest Appeal Court in the land.

✚ 137 B7 ✉ Public entrance on St Margaret Street
☎ Information Office 020 7219 3000 (Commons), 020 7219 3107 (Lords); summer tours 0870 906 3773 ◉ The public may attend debates when the Houses are sitting ✋ Free; summer tours expensive ◉ Westminster 🚌 3, 11, 12, 24, 53, 77a, 211, 453 🚆 Waterloo

4 National Gallery

www.nationalgallery.org.uk

Home to one of the finest and most extensive collections of Western art in the world, the National Gallery houses more than 2,000 paintings.

The collection is divided chronologically, with the Sainsbury Wing housing the oldest paintings, from 1260 to 1510. Two of the most famous works are *The Virgin and Child* cartoon by Leonardo da Vinci and *Venus and Mars* by Botticelli. *The Doge* by Giovanni Bellini is widely considered the greatest Venetian portrait. Less famous but equally worthwhile are *The Wilton Diptych* (by an unknown artist), *The Battle of San Romano* by Uccello, *The Baptism of Christ* by Piero della Francesca and *The Arnolfini Portrait* by Jan van Eyck.

The West Wing progresses to 1600 and includes *The Entombment* (unfinished) by Michelangelo. Two famous mythology paintings are *Bacchus and Ariadne* by Titian and *Allegory with Venus and Cupid* by Bronzino. More 'worldly' masterpieces include Holbein's *Ambassadors* and *Pope Julius II* by Raphael.

The North Wing deals with the 17th century. Among its 15 or so Rembrandts is the sorrowful *Self Portrait at the Age of 63* (that same year he died a pauper). Contrast this

with the pompous *Equestrian Portrait of Charles I* by Van Dyck, and the charming *Le Chapeau de Paille* (Straw Hat) portrait by Rubens. *Young Woman Standing at a Virginal* by Vermeer, *The Rokeby Venus* by Velázquez and *Enchanted Castle* by Claude are also worth seeking out.

The East Wing (1700–1900) contains a whole host of popular favourites: *Sunflowers* by Van Gogh; *Bathers at Asnières* by Seurat; *Gare St-Lazare* by Monet; and from the British school, *The Hay Wain* by Constable and *Fighting Temeraire* by Turner.

➕ 131 F6 ✉ Trafalgar Square ☎ 020 7747 2885 🕐 Daily 10–6 (Wed until 9). Closed 24–26 Dec, 1 Jan ✋ Free 🍴 Café (£), brasserie (££) Ⓔ Charing Cross, Leicester Square 🚌 3, 6, 9, 11, 12, 13, 15, 23, 24, 29, 53, 77a, 88, 91, 139, 159, 176, 453 🚆 Charing Cross ℹ Lower Regent Street

5 Natural History Museum

www.nhm.ac.uk

A family favourite where dinosaurs roar back to life, an earthquake shakes the ground and creepy-crawlies make the flesh tingle.

To thousands of children the Natural History Museum is 'the Dinosaur Museum', and no visit would be complete without poring over the superbly displayed skeletons of the museum's world-famous collection. There's much more here than just prehistoric monsters, however. Highest of all on the heavyweights list is the blue whale. It may only be a model, but what a model, measuring over 28m (92ft) with a real 25m (82ft) skeleton alongside. Around here there is a vast array of mammal specimens to ponder while at the other end of the size spectrum, children (if not adults) will love the 'Creepy-crawlies' exhibition. For more ethereal concepts, visit the state-of-the-art Ecology display and gingerly examine the workings of your own body in the Human Biology section. One of the museum's greatest attractions is its very structure, designed in neo-Gothic cathedral style by Alfred Waterhouse in 1880. The Cromwell Road façade is magnificent and there is a wealth of interior detail to enjoy.

Once you've seen life on earth, explore the adjacent Earth Galleries (formerly known as the Geological Museum), which tell the story of the earth's formation and its ongoing upheavals. This is

a far cry from the old museum's displays of rocks in dusty glass cases, though its collection of gemstones remains a highlight. The main attraction is The Power Within exhibitions, where the ground-shaking sensations of a real earthquake are simulated and audio-visuals show incredible footage of volcanoes and their devastating effects on everyday objects.

🚹 135 C6 ✉ Cromwell Road (Life Galleries), Exhibition Road (Earth Galleries) ☎ 020 7942 5000 🕐 Daily 10–5:50. Last admission 5:30. Closed 24–26 Dec 🖐 Free 🍴 Restaurant (££) and cafés (£) 🚇 South Kensington 🚌 74

❓ Explore tour: daily 45 mins long. Reserve on the day at the information desk or call 020 7942 5011. Free

6 St Paul's Cathedral

www.stpauls.co.uk

The Mother Church of the Diocese of London and the supreme work of Sir Christopher Wren, one of the world's great architects.

Work began on the present St Paul's Cathedral after the Great Fire of 1666 had destroyed its predecessor, Old St Paul's. Its foundation stone was laid by Christopher Wren in 1675 and after 35 years of sweat and toil (during which time Wren's salary was halved as punishment for slow progress) it was completed in 1710. Take time to enjoy the magnificent west front before entering the church. Inside it is surprisingly light and airy, largely as a result of the use of plain glass windows (much favoured by Wren), which were installed to replace the old stained glass ones that were destroyed during World War II.

Go past the huge monument to the Duke of Wellington and stop in the middle of the transepts to look skywards to the wonderful dome – one of the three largest in the world. Move on to the choir, the most lavishly decorated part of the church, and don't miss the scorch-marked statue of John Donne (poet and Dean of Old St Paul's). This is one of London's very few monuments to survive the Great Fire of 1666.

Descend to the crypt, where you will find the tombs of some of Britain's greatest heroes, including the Duke of Wellington and Lord Nelson, and, of course, Christopher Wren himself. Return to the church and begin the ascent to the galleries. The justifiably famous Whispering Gallery, whose remarkable acoustics will carry a whisper quite audibly from one side to the other, is perched 30m (98ft) above the floor. Finally, after a total of 530 steps, you will reach the Golden Gallery, where you

will be rewarded with one of the finest views in all London. Return to the cathedral floor and contemplate William Holman Hunt's uplifting masterpiece, *The Light of the World*.

🔢 132 E3 ✉ St Paul's Churchyard
☎ 020 7236 4128 🕐 Mon–Sat
8:30–4:30 (last admission 4)
💷 Expensive, includes cathedral, crypt
and climbing galleries 🍽 Refectory
Restaurant (£); Café in crypt (£) 🚇 St
Paul's 🚌 11, 15, 23, 26, 100 🚉 St Paul's,
City Thameslink ❓ Self-guided audio
tours, 90-min guided tours

7 Science Museum

www.sciencemuseum.org.uk

Don't be put off by the name or the concept of a museum of science. This is an exhibition of how things work and how technology has evolved.

The Science Museum is one of the world's finest collections of its kind. It is a huge undertaking, and you can't hope to see everything here in a single visit. On the other hand there are so many pieces that are landmarks of industrial history, technological milestones, works of art, or just amazing objects in their own right, there really is something that everyone can identify with and admire.

To see the best of the collection in one visit buy the excellent museum guidebook, which will navigate you through the 'must-see' exhibits such as Stephenson's *Rocket*, Edison's early lamps, the ill-fated Ford Edsel motorcar, the prototype computer (the dauntingly huge Babbage's Difference Engine), the Apollo 10 Command module, the first iron lung and many other famous technological landmarks.

The Science Museum is famous for its pioneering interactive hands-on areas and adults with children should start down in the basement, then progress to the Launch Pad. Here youngsters can discover how machines and gadgets work. Other family favourites include the Flight Galleries, featuring a whole array of historic aircraft, many of them slung dramatically from the ceiling. For sheer spectacle it's hard to beat the East Hall, where some of the great beam-and-steam behemoths that powered the Industrial Revolution still push and thrust their mighty workings.

The Wellcome History of Medicine, on the top floor, is a fascinating collection with an emphasis on ancient and tribal medicines.

✚ 135 C6 ✉ Exhibition Road ☎ 0870 870 4868 🕐 Daily 10–6. Closed 24–26 Dec ✋ Free 🍴 Restaurants (£), café (£), picnic areas Ⓤ South Kensington 🚌 9, 10, 14, 49, 52, 70, 74, 345, 360, 414, C1 ❓ IMAX cinema (expensive); simulators (inexpensive–moderate)

8 Tower of London

www.hrp.org.uk

London's foremost historical site, the Tower has served as castle, palace, prison, arsenal, jewel house and site of execution over its 900-year lifespan.

The oldest part of the Tower of London is the great central keep. Known as the White Tower, it was begun by William I in 1078 to intimidate his newly

ENTRY TO THE TRAITORS GATE

conquered subjects; the rest of the fortifications took on their present shape in the late 13th and early 14th centuries.

All tours begin with an hour-long, highly entertaining guided walk led by one of the Tower's traditionally dressed Yeoman Warders (Beefeaters). They gleefully relate stories of imprisonment, torture and intrigue – later on you can check out the Torture in the Tower exhibition for further gruesome details – while taking you past a few of the 20 towers, the famous ravens ('only so long as they stay will the White Tower stand'), Traitors' Gate and the execution site of Tower Green. Here, among others, Henry VIII's wives Anne Boleyn and Catherine Howard lost their heads.

After visiting the adjacent Chapel of St Peter ad Vincula you are left to explore by yourself and join the inevitable queues at the Jewel House and the White Tower. Both are well worth the wait. The former houses the Crown Jewels, many of which date back to the 17th-century Restoration period and are still used by the present Queen and royal family. The White Tower is home to the beautiful 11th-century Chapel of St John. Also highly recommended is a visit to the restored rooms of the medieval palace.

✚ 133 F6 ✉ Tower of London ☎ 0870 756 6060
🕐 Mar–Oct Tue–Sat 9–6, Sun, Mon 10–6 (last admission 5); Nov–Feb Tue–Sat 9–5, Sun–Mon 10–5 (last admission 4). Closed 24–26 Dec, 1 Jan 👆 Expensive 🍴 Café (£), restaurant (£) 🚇 Tower Hill 🚌 15, 42, 78, 100, D1
🚉 Street, London Bridge ❓ Buy tickets in advance online or from any underground station to avoid waiting at entrance

9 Victoria and Albert Museum

www.vam.ac.uk

The V&A is Britain's national museum of art and design, and contains the greatest collection of decorative arts in the world.

The V&A was founded in 1852 with the objective of exhibiting the world's very best examples of design and applied arts in order to inspire students and craftspeople. It has subsequently grown to include an astonishing and immense diversity of objects. Your first task is to arm yourself with a map and index to help you navigate the 13km (8 miles) labyrinth of stairs and corridors.

Perhaps the V&A's greatest treasures are the Raphael Cartoons, seven huge tapestry designs that have become even more famous than the actual tapestries themselves (which hang in the Sistine Chapel in Rome). While on the ground floor,

don't miss the Italian Renaissance sculptures; the Cast Courts, full-size plaster casts of fascinating European masterpieces including Trajan's Column and Michelangelo's *David*; and the Morris, Poynter and Gamble Rooms, the V&A's original refreshment rooms and masterpieces of Victorian decoration. Dip into the treasures of the Orient from China, Japan, the Muslim world and India – don't miss Tipoo's Tiger, one of the museum's most famous pieces – and the Fashion collections.

Look for the Glass Gallery, a wonderful exhibition of glass spanning a period of 4,000 years. See the lavishly refurbished British Galleries and the Silver Galleries, the culmination of an eight-year V&A project. Tucked away in the Paintings Galleries are some of John Constable's best works.

The Jameel Gallery opened in 2006, displaying a superb Islamic collection.

🚪 135 C7 ✉ Entrances on Exhibition Road, Cromwell Road ☎ 020 7942 2000; 0870 442 0808 for recorded information 🕐 Daily 10–5:45. Wed and last Fri of month 10–10. Closed 24–26, 31 Dec, 1 Jan 💷 Free 🍴 Excellent cafés (£) and restaurant (££) on premises 🚇 South Kensington 🚌 C1, 14, 74 stop outside Cromwell Road entrance ❓ Tours: introductory tours daily (lasting 1 hour) hourly 10:30–3:30

10 Westminster Abbey

www.westminster-abbey.org

The coronation site of British royalty, the last resting place of kings, queens and celebrities, this architectural triumph is awash with history.

Westminster Abbey was founded c1050 by Edward the Confessor, who was the first king to be buried here. William the Conqueror was crowned king in the abbey on Christmas Day in 1066 and so began a tradition that was last re-enacted in 1953 when the coronation of the present monarch, Queen Elizabeth II, took place here.

The present building dates mostly from the 13th century and the reign of Henry III. The nave is full of graves and monuments, none more famous

than the Tomb of the Unknown Warrior, who represents the 765,000 British servicemen killed in World War I, though the real glory of the abbey lies beyond the sumptuously carved and gilded screen (by which Isaac Newton and Charles Darwin lie) in the Royal Chapels. Here you will find the coronation chair and the often magnificent tombs of dozens of royals.

The abbey's *tour de force* lies at its easternmost point; Henry VII's Chapel, built

between 1503 and 1519, with its sublime fan-vaulting. In the south transept is the famous Poets' Corner where many celebrated writers, musicians and artists are honoured.

Try to see the beautiful abbey precinct that includes the cloisters, the Westminster Abbey Museum (with contemporary royal wax effigies), the Chapter House and the Pyx ('money chest') Chamber (reopened after restoration).

✚ 137 B6 ✉ Dean's Yard, Broad Sanctuary ☎ Abbey 020 7654 4900 🕐 Nave, cloisters daily 8–6; abbey Mon–Fri 9:30–4:45 (Wed 9:30–7), Sat 9–2:45. Last admission 1 hour before closing time. No sightseeing on Sun; Pyx Chamber, Chapter House and museum daily 10:30–4 🎫 Cloisters free; abbey expensive, includes Chapter House, museum, Pyx Chamber 🍴 Coffee stands outside abbey and in cloister 🚇 Westminster, St James's Park 🚌 3, 11, 24, 53, 77a, 159, 211 ❓ Guided tours: Apr–Sep Mon–Fri 10, 10:30, 11, 2, 2:30; Sat 10, 10:30, 11; Oct–Mar Mon–Fri 10:30, 11, 2, 2:30; Sat 10:30, 11 ☎ Reserve tours in advance 020 7654 4900 🎫 Moderate; audio tour available Mon–Fri 9:30–3, Sat 9:30–1 🎫 Inexpensive–moderate

Exploring

St James's, Mayfair and Piccadilly

If you only had one day in the city this area, between Buckingham Palace and Trafalgar Square, is full of highlights and gives an insight into traditional, quintessential London.

MAYFAIR

ST JAMES'S

The wealthy district contains some of the city's grandest architecture, leafy squares and pretty parks, as well as exclusive shopping opportunities. Buckingham Palace, the Queen's official London residence, sits at the end of the grand, tree-lined processional Mall and is at the top of the list for many visitors, particularly for the famous Changing of the Guard ceremony. Not far away is the much older St James's Palace and adjacent is Clarence House, London home of Prince Charles and the Duchess of Cornwall.

For relaxation stroll through St James's Park or Green Park; both are welcome oases in a busy city. The area's elegance and refinement make it unique in the capital. You can visit the Royal

Academy and the smart shops and arcades of Piccadilly, one of London's great thoroughfares. In Trafalgar Square – known worldwide for Nelson's Column – is the National Gallery, home to the country's premier art collection.

BANQUETING HOUSE

Banqueting House is the only surviving part of Henry VIII's great Whitehall Palace, which burned down in 1698. Designed in classical style by Inigo Jones, it was completed in 1622 and is famous for its magnificent ceiling painting by Rubens. This huge work was commissioned by Charles I to celebrate the wisdom of the reign of the Stuart dynasty and depicts his father, James I. It was therefore to provide an ironic backdrop to the events of 30 January 1649 when Charles, defeated in the English Civil War, stepped out from a window of

Banqueting House on to a scaffold to face the executioner's axe. The vaulted undercroft (crypt), formerly the wine cellar of James I, is also open to the public.

www.hrp.org.uk

✚ 137 A6 ✉ Whitehall ☎ 0870 751 5178
🕒 Mon–Sat 10–5. Closed 24 Dec–1 Jan, Good Fri, all public hols and for functions at short notice
✋ Moderate 🍴 Café-in-the-Crypt, St. Martin-in-the-Fields, Trafalgar Square (£) 🚇 Westminster, Embankment

BUCKINGHAM PALACE

World-famous as the London home of the Queen, this vast, sprawling, 775-room house was built mostly between 1820 and 1837, although the familiar East Front public face of the palace was not added until 1913. Buckingham Palace has been opening its doors to the public since 1993, with proceeds going towards the restoration of Windsor Castle (➤ 122). Visitors get to view the **State Rooms,** which are furnished with some of the most important works of art from the Royal Collection – one of the largest and most valuable private art collections in the world. There's no chance of spotting any of the royal family, however, as they are always away when the palace is open.

Around the corner, on Buckingham Palace Road is the **Queen's Gallery,** which reopened for the Queen's Gold Jubilee in 2002 and exhibits items from the Royal Collection. Alongside is the **Royal Mews,** where, among the horses and tack, is a display of the opulent carriages that are wheeled out on state occasions.

The Changing of the Guard is still the most popular reason for visiting the palace. It takes place daily from May to July and on alternate days the rest of the year (weather permitting). At around 11.15 the St James's Palace part of the old guard marches down the Mall to meet the old guard of Buckingham Palace. There they await the arrival, at 11:30, of the new guard from Wellington

Barracks, who are accompanied by a band. Keys are ceremonially handed from the old to the new guard while the band plays. When the sentries have been changed, at around 12:05, the old guard returns to Wellington Barracks and the new part of the St James's Palace guard marches off to St James's Palace. As it can be extremely busy, aim to get close to the railings well before 11, particularly in high summer.

www.royal.gov.uk

➕ 136 B4 ✉ The Mall ☎ 020 7766 7300

State Rooms

✉ Buckingham Palace ⊘ Tours daily Aug–Sep 9:30–4:15 (last tour) ✋ Very expensive ⓖ Green Park, Hyde Park Corner, St James's Park, Victoria
❓ Tickets from Green Park office on day of visit or in advance by credit card
☎ 020 7766 7300

Queen's Gallery

✉ Buckingham Palace Road ☎ 020 7321 2233 ⊘ Daily 10–5:30 (last admission 4:30) ✋ Expensive

Royal Mews

✉ Buckingham Palace Road ☎ 020 7766 7302 ⊘ Aug–Sep daily 10–5; Oct–Jul daily 11–4 (last admission 45 mins before closing) ✋ Expensive
ⓖ Hyde Park Corner, St James's Park, Victoria

CABINET WAR ROOMS AND CHURCHILL MUSEUM

This underground warren of rooms provided secure accommodation for the War Cabinet and their military advisers during World War II and was used on over 100 occasions. Today it is a time capsule, with the clocks stopped at 4:58pm on 15 October 1940 and the ghost of Winston Churchill hanging heavy in the air. You can view his private kitchen, dining room and his wife's bedroom. Many of his speeches were made from here and some are played to heighten the evocative atmosphere.

www.iwm.org.uk

✚ 137 B6 ✉ Clive Steps, King Charles Street ☎ 020 7930 6961 ⊘ Daily 9:30–6 (last admission 5). Closed 24–26 Dec ✋ Expensive (under 16 free) 🍴 Switchroom Café (£) Ⓢ Westminster ❓ Admission includes audio guide

JERMYN STREET

Jermyn (pronounced German) Street is a slice of traditional 'Gentleman's London', famous for its exclusive and elegant shops. Cigar-smokers should look in at Davidoff, while pipe-smokers will enjoy Dunhill. Don't miss Floris (at No 89), Paxton & Whitfield (No 93) and Bates the Hatter (No 21a) featuring Binks the cat, stuffed in 1926, in a black top hat.

✚ 131 F5 Ⓢ Green Park, Piccadilly Circus

NATIONAL GALLERY

Best places to see, pages 28–29.

NATIONAL PORTRAIT GALLERY

Founded in 1856 as the 'Gallery of the Portraits of the most eminent persons in British History', the gallery's earliest contemporary portrait is that of Henry VII, from 1505. If you want to see the exhibits in chronological order go up to the top floor and work your way down. The collection is too large to be displayed at one time so it changes periodically. The pictures least likely to change are the oldest, many of which are of great historical value. Those most likely to be rotated are the portraits of late 20th-century figures; the display of new additions tends to be dictated by current public interest.

Most visitors' favourites are the very earliest (top floor), the most recent, the Victorian and the early 20th century galleries. Predictably, there are many images of royalty, and at opposite ends of the gallery is a wonderful contrast of styles featuring the likenesses of Elizabeth I and, some 400 years later, the present British queen, Elizabeth II. The Coronation Portrait of Elizabeth I is an acclaimed masterpiece, while much more controversial is the colour screenprint, in signature fashion by Andy Warhol, of the current monarch. This also underlines the point that the gallery holds more than just conventional paintings; sculptures, photography, sketches, silhouettes, caricatures and other methods of portraiture are all featured. Among contemporary portraits you'll find soccer star David Beckham, musician Sir Paul McCartney and actors Sir Ian McKellen and Catherine Zeta-Jones.

www.npg.org.uk

➕ 131 F6 ✉ St Martin's Place, Orange Street ☎ 020 7306 0055 🕐 Daily 10–6 (Thu, Fri until 9). Closed 24–26 Dec 🖐 Free (except special exhibitions) 🍴 Rooftop restaurant (££), café (£) 🚇 Leicester Square, Charing Cross ❓ Audio guides to over 350 portraits; frequent lectures and tours

PICCADILLY CIRCUS

London's most famous circus (a site where several streets meet) is almost permanently clogged with traffic and young tourists who use the steps around the Statue of Eros as a convenient rest stop or meeting point. The statue actually represents the Angel of Christian Charity, not the Greek God of love. Piccadilly Circus is a frenetic, unattractive place, best seen at night when the illuminated billboards come to life. Just off here is the rather tacky Trocadero, claimed to be Europe's largest indoor entertainment complex.

✚ 131 F5 🚇 Piccadilly Circus

ROYAL ACADEMY OF ARTS

The RA is the country's oldest fine arts society and regularly stages world-class art exhibitions, most famously the annual Summer Exhibition (in June). The elegant home of the RA, Burlington House, features some fine 18th-century ceiling paintings and has opened its Fine Rooms to provide a permanent display space. This includes major works by leading British artists from Reynolds to Hockney, plus Britain's sole Michelangelo sculpture.

www.royalacademy.org.uk

➕ 130 F4 ✉ Burlington House, Piccadilly ☎ 020 7300 8000. Advance tickets 0870 848 8484 ◷ Daily during exhibition 10–6 (Fri until 10). Fine Rooms Tue–Fri 1–4:30; Sat, Sun 10–6. Closed 25 Dec ✋ Expensive; Fine Rooms – depends on exhibition 🍴 Café (£), buffet restaurant (££) Ⓤ Green Park, Piccadilly Circus

ST JAMES'S CHURCH

This 'little piece of heaven in Piccadilly' was built between 1676 and 1684 by Christopher Wren, though it was badly damaged in World War II and has largely been rebuilt. The main artistic interest of the church is the work of Grinling Gibbons, the greatest woodcarver in 17th-century England. However, the church's popularity, particularly with local Londoners, lies in the numerous cultural activities it promotes, including an arts and crafts market, an antiques market and regular top-class concerts and recitals.

www.st-james-piccadilly.org

🚹 131 F5 ✉ 197 Piccadilly ☎ 020 7734 4511 🕐 Daily 8–6:30 💷 Free
🍴 Café (£) 🚇 Green Park, Piccadilly Circus ❓ Concerts, recitals: Mon, Wed, Fri at 1:10 (free).

Evening concerts usually Thu, Fri, Sat 7:30 (expensive). Craft market Wed–Sat 11–7; antiques market Tue 10–6

ST JAMES'S PALACE

After the Palace of Whitehall was destroyed in 1698, the court moved to St James's Palace, which remained the official royal London residence until 1837, when Queen Victoria decamped to Buckingham Palace. Sadly, little remains of the palace's Tudor structure except for the splendid main gatehouse in Pall Mall. The Chapel Royal also retains its original exterior. Adjacent to the palace is **Clarence House,** formerly home to the late Queen Mother, but now occupied by the Prince of Wales. It is now open to the public for a short period during the summer.

www.royal.gov.uk

🚹 137 A5 ✉ Chapel Royal, St James's Palace 🕐 Open for services only (see notice board on door to confirm; not Aug and Sep) 💷 Free 🍴 Inn the Park (£–££) 🚇 Green Park

Clarence House

☎ 020 7766 7303 🕐 Aug to early Oct daily 9:30–4 by guided tour only
💷 Moderate

ST JAMES'S PARK

The oldest and the prettiest of central London's royal parks, St James's was established by Henry VIII in the 1530s. Don't miss the magical views from the bridge in the centre of the lake, west to Buckingham Palace and east to the domes and towers of Whitehall.

✚ 137 A5 ✋ Free 🚇 St James's Park

ST JAMES'S STREET

St James's is 'Gentlemen's London' and here you will find four of its most distinguished clubs: White's (No 37–8), where Prince Charles held his stag party in 1981; Boodle's (No 28), haunt of London's chief 19th-century dandy, Beau Brummell; Brooks's (No 60), renowned for its gambling; and the Carlton (No 69), bastion of the

Conservative party, whose male-only rules were bent for Mrs Thatcher when she was Prime Minister. Admission to all clubs is by membership only.

Of more general interest are three of London's most intriguing small shops. John Lobb's at No 9 was established in 1849 and has been 'bootmakers to the Crown' since 1911. Look inside the shop's small museum case for historical items such as the wooden last that was used for Queen Victoria's shoes. At No 6 is James Lock & Co, the 'most famous hat shop in the world', which has provided headwear for national heroes such as Nelson and Wellington and where the bowler hat was invented. The picturesque early 19th-century premises of wine merchants Berry Brothers & Rudd are at No 3, adjacent to a narrow alley leading to tiny Pickering Place where, between 1842 and 1845, the Republic of Texas kept a legation (diplomatic ministry).

✠ 136 A4 🚇 Green Park

SPENCER HOUSE

Built between 1756 and 1766 for Earl Spencer (an ancestor of the late Diana, Princess of Wales), Spencer House is London's finest surviving mid-18th century house. After being completely restored at a cost of £16 million, it was opened to visitors in 1990. The one-hour guided tour takes in eight rooms featuring elegant gilded decorations and period paintings and furniture.

www.spencerhouse.co.uk

✠ 136 A4 ✉ 27 St James's Place ☎ 020 7499 8620 🕐 Sun 10:30–4:45. Closed Jan, Aug. Access by 1-hour tour only 👜 Expensive 🍴 Quaglinos (£££) 🚇 Green Park ❓ No children under 10

TRAFALGAR SQUARE

This is the geographical and symbolic centre of London; all road distances are measured from here and at its heart is Nelson's Column. The buildings of South Africa House, Canada House and the National Gallery line three sides of the square, while the fourth opens to Whitehall. The square takes its name from the Battle of Trafalgar in 1805, during which Admiral Nelson, Britain's greatest naval hero, commanded his fleet to the famous victory against Franco-Spanish forces. Nelson was killed during the battle and the column, 57m (187ft) high, was erected between 1839 and 1842.

The church on the square, with its tower dramatically floodlit by night, is **St Martin-in-the-Fields,** built in 1726 by James Gibbs. This handsome building is famous for concerts and is also a thriving community centre with a social care unit and several minor visitor attractions. Above ground it hosts a daily clothes and crafts market, while its famous crypt houses an art gallery, the London Brass Rubbing Centre, gift shops and the excellent Café-in-the-Crypt.
www.stmartin-in-the-fields.org

✚ 131 F6

St Martin-in-the-Fields

✉ Trafalgar Square ☎ General enquiries 020 7766 1100; concert enquiries 020 7839 8362 ◑ Church: Mon–Sat 8–6:30, Sun 8–7:30. Crypt brass rubbing centre Mon–Wed 10–7, Thu–Sat 10–10, Sun 12–7. Concerts: Mon, Tue, Fri at 1pm. Candlelit concerts of baroque music: most Tue, Thu–Sat 7:30 ✋ Free. Lunchtime concerts donation, evening concerts expensive 🍴 Café-in-the-Crypt (£) Ⓔ Charing Cross, Leicester Square

WHITEHALL

Whitehall has been the country's principal corridor of power since the early 18th century. The epicentre is Downing Street, home to the Prime Minister and to the Chancellor of the Exchequer, while north and south are various grey and sober buildings that house the country's top civil servants and ministries. Just south of Downing Street is the Cenotaph, the national memorial to the dead of the two World Wars. The street was named after Henry VIII's Whitehall Palace, which burned down in 1698, leaving Banqueting House (► 46) as the sole surviving building above ground. Opposite here is Horse Guards, the historic, official entrance to the royal palaces, still guarded by two mounted troopers and a good place to watch one of London's guard-changing ceremonies.

✚ 137 A6 🚫 No public access to Downing Street 🍴 Café-in-the-Crypt 🚇 South end Westminster; north end Charing Cross
❓ Horse Guards guard changes 11am Mon–Sat, 10am Sun; ceremonial dismounting and inspection daily at 4. National Remembrance Service held at the Cenotaph at 11am on Sun nearest 11 Nov

The City and East

The City of London, the heart and financial centre of the old capital, is one of the busiest commercial hubs in the world, with banks, corporate headquarters and insurance companies occupying dramatic showcases of modern architecture. Yet alongside these, you find sublime 17th-century churches, cobbled alleyways, historic markets and fragments of the original Roman city wall.

Much of the medieval city was destroyed in the Great Fire of 1666, and in the construction that followed as many as 50 Wren churches were built. Three of London's most iconic sights – St Paul's Cathedral, the Tower of London and London Bridge – are in this district. The City of London is home to the modern Barbican Centre, a performing arts venue, and to the Museum of London, where the story of the capital is brought to life. To the west are four historic Inns of Court, the heart of legal London. Stretching downstream to the east lies Docklands, a huge area of urban redevelopment. Here is a vibrant, diverse and culturally interesting area with historic warehouses, riverside pubs and restaurants, as well as opportunities for watersports.

BANK OF ENGLAND MUSEUM

The story of Britain's monetary and banking system since 1604 is told at this museum. The Bank of England is the nation's central bank, functioning at the heart of one of the world's largest and most sophisicated financial centres. A visit to this small but lively museum will enlighten you as to its workings and its history. Having been in existence so long, the bank has accumulated a considerable number of items associated with its history. The collections include banknotes and coins, furniture, books, pictures and statues. Highlights are its real gold bullion (each house-brick-sized bar is worth around £70,000), the reproduction banking hall and the award-winning interactive screens and currency dealing computer game.

www.bankofengland.co.uk/museum

➕ 133 A5 ✉ Bartholomew Lane ☎ 020 7601 5545 🕐 Mon–Fri 10–5
✋ Free 🍴 Sweetings (££), 39 Queen Victoria Street, The City Ⓜ Bank

COURTAULD GALLERY

The Courtauld Gallery has been called the greatest concentration of Western European art anywhere in the world and features a great collection of Impressionist paintings. It is housed in Somerset House, one of the finest and most important 18th-century public buildings in London.

The Impressionists and Post-Impressionists are top priority, particularly Van Gogh's *Self Portrait with Bandaged Ear* and Manet's *Bar at the Folies Bergère*. Other paintings include *Le Déjeuner sur l'Herbe*, also by Manet, *The Card Players* by Cézanne, *La Loge* by Renoir, *Two Dancers on a Stage* by Degas and Gauguin's Tahitian works. The collection goes back to the 15th century, and early masterpieces include works by Cranach the Elder, a superb Holy Trinity by Botticelli and from the early 17th century a large number

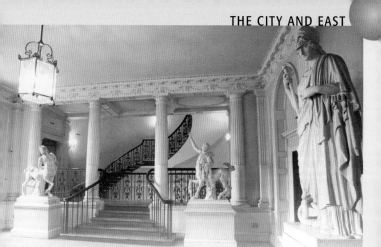

of paintings by Rubens. There are also some fine 20th-century works.

www.courtauld.ac.uk/gallery

🏛 131 E8 ✉ Somerset House, Strand ☎ 020 7848 2526 🕐 Daily 10–6 (last admission 5:15) 👋 Moderate; children free. Free Mon 10–2 (except public hols) 🍴 Gallery Café (£) 🚇 Temple (closed Sun), Covent Garden, Holborn

DICKENS HOUSE MUSEUM

Dating from 1801, this elegant residence is the only surviving house in which Charles Dickens lived for any length of time while in London. He stayed here from April 1837 to December 1839, long enough to secure his burgeoning reputation by writing the final instalments of *The Pickwick Papers*, almost all of *Oliver Twist*, the whole of *Nicholas Nickleby* and the start of *Barnaby Rudge*. Opened as a museum in 1925, the house now holds the finest collection of Dickens memorabilia in existence, with many of the exhibits reflecting the novels that were written here.

www.dickensmuseum.com

🏛 131 B8 ✉ 48 Doughty Street ☎ 020 7405 2127 🕐 Mon–Sat 10–5, Sun 11–5 (last admission 4:30) 👋 Moderate 🍴 The Lamb (£) 🚇 Russell Square, Chancery Lane

DOCKLANDS

London's Docklands stretch some 8km
(5 miles) east of the Tower of London to
the old Royal Docks. Historically, this area
was the powerhouse of the Empire, at its
height the busiest port in the world. It
reached the peak of its activity in 1964 but
changes in technology (most notably
containerization) signalled its sudden
demise. Within a decade most of the
quays and great swathes of nearby land
were derelict and remained so until the
early 1980s when the government began
the world's largest urban redevelopment
project to date. For an excellent insight into
the area's rich history visit the Museum in
Docklands, West India Quay (daily 10–6).

The centrepiece is Canary Wharf,
Britain's tallest building at 243m (797ft).
A trip on the Docklands Light Railway is
recommended for its high-level views into this Brave New London
World. The latest DLR line, to London City Airport, opened in 2005.
Try also the area's historical riverside pubs, which include the
Prospect of Whitby, the Mayflower and the Grapes.
www.museumindocklands.org
✚ 140 D2

FLEET STREET

Fleet Street became the original publishing centre of London in
1500, when England's first press was set up here. From 1702 until
the 1980s it was also the home of England's newspapers until
new technology meant they could decamp to cheaper, more
efficient offices away from the Street of Ink. Today it is still worth a
visit for St Bride's Church (▶ 70) and the little alleyways that run

north of here. Wine Office Court is home to Ye Olde Cheshire Cheese pub, while close by is **Dr Johnson's House,** built around 1700 and now a museum dedicated to the writer who gave us the first English dictionary.

Dr Johnson's House

✚ 132 E1 ✉ 17 Gough Square ☎ 020 7353 3745; www.drjohnsonshouse.org ⏱ Mon–Sat 11–5:30, (Oct–Apr 11–5). Closed 22 Dec–2 Jan 💷 Moderate
🍴 Ye Olde Cheshire Cheese 🚇 Chancery Lane, Blackfriars

GUILDHALL

The City of London has been governed from this site for over 800 years and the majestic centrepiece of the Great Hall dates back to 1430. Its huge crypt is older, dating from the mid-13th century, and even older are the excavated remains of London's only Roman amphitheatre. The banners and stained-glass coats of arms that

decorate the hall belong to the City Livery companies, formed in medieval times to represent and support their professions, and still in existence today. Within the complex is a Clock Museum and the Guildhall Art Gallery featuring 300 years of London art.

www.cityoflondon.gov.uk

✚ 132 D4 ✉ Guildhall, Gresham Street
☎ 020 7606 3030 ⏱ Great Hall and amphitheatre Mon–Sat 10–5. Closed for ceremonies and events. Art Gallery Mon–Sat 10–5, Sun 12–4. Clock Museum Mon–Sat 9:30–4:45 ☎ 020 7332 1868 💷 Great Hall, amphitheatre, Clock Museum free; art gallery inexpensive (free all day Fri and after 3:30 on other days) 🍴 The Place Below (£), St Mary-le-Bow Church, Cheapside 🚇 Bank, St Paul's, Mansion House

INNS OF COURT

The Inns of Court, the training grounds for the country's barristers (lawyers), date from medieval times. Today only four survive: Inner Temple, Middle Temple, Lincoln's Inn and Gray's Inn. Each resembles a small college campus, with a library, chapel, hall and barristers' chambers. Their grounds, usually open Monday to Friday, are central London's most charming and peaceful oases, and their narrow alleyways and small courtyards, many still gaslit, are very atmospheric in the early evening (➤ 66–67).

🔢 131 E8 🖐 Free 🚇 Temple, Holborn, Chancery Lane

LLOYD'S BUILDING

Designed by Richard Rogers, of Georges Pompidou Centre (Paris) fame, and sharing the same characteristic of wearing its guts on its sleeve, this stunning glass and steel tower ('a post-modern oil refinery' said one critic) was the most controversial building in England when finished in 1986. It is closed to the public but remains one of London's most potent architectural statements.

🔢 133 E6 ✉ Leadenhall Street 🚫 Closed to public 🍴 Leadenhall Wine & Tapas Bar (£), Leadenhall Market 🚇 Aldgate

MONUMENT

Monument is the world's highest free-standing column; it measures 62m (203ft), which is exactly the distance, due east of the site, of the bakery in Pudding Lane where the Great Fire of London began in 1666. It was commissioned by King Charles II and designed by Christopher Wren and Robert Hooke. You can climb inside the column via a 311-step spiral staircase and enjoy views of the City.

🔢 133 E5 ✉ Monument Street ☎ 020 7626 2717 🚫 Daily 9:30–5 🖐 Inexpensive 🍴 Leadenhall Wine & Tapas Bar (£), Leadenhall Market 🚇 Monument

a walk around the Inns of Court

This walk should be done on a weekday because not only is the area deserted and devoid of atmosphere at weekends, but several areas within the Inns are closed.

Turn left out of Temple underground station, go up the steps and turn right into Temple Place, which leads (via a car park entrance) to Inner Temple. Turn left up steps to Fountain Court.

The splendid Elizabethan hall and the adjacent gardens are occasionally open.

Continue straight on beneath the archway following the sign to Lamb's Buildings into Middle Temple. Go up the steps to the left of the building ahead to find Temple Church, built in 1185 and famous for its effigies of 13th-

century Crusader knights. Leave Temple by the alleyway adjacent to Dr Johnson's Buildings.

At the end is the doorway to Prince Henry's Room, a rare Elizabethan survivor with a fine 17th-century interior.

Cross Fleet Street, turn left, then right alongside the monumental Royal Courts of Justice into Bell Yard. At the end turn left and, by Legastat printers, turn right into New Square, heart of Lincoln's Inn.

Lincoln's Inn's splendid hall (left) isn't open but you can visit the chapel (right, open 12–2:30 on weekdays), built in 1620.

Continue through the Inn and exit right at the corner of Stone Buildings. Cross Chancery Lane, turn right, then go left into Southampton Buildings, which leads to Staple Inn.

This is a former Inn of Chancery (a prep school for the Inns of Court); note its Elizabethan façade on High Holborn.

Cross High Holborn, turn left, then, by the Cittie of York pub, go right into Gray's Inn. Duck beneath the arch to the left of the hall (closed) to Gray's Inn Gardens. Return to High Holborn for Chancery Lane tube.

Distance Approximately 4km (2.5 miles)
Time 2–3 hours depending on visits
Start point 🚇 Temple (closed Sun) ✚ 132 E1
End point 🚇 Chancery Lane (closed Sun) ✚ 132 D1
Lunch Cittie of York, Holborn (£)

MUSEUM OF LONDON

Reputed to be the most comprehensive city museum in the world, the multi-award-winning Museum of London tells you everything you ever wanted to know about the history of the capital. The displays are engaging and the captions punchy and entertaining. There's a lot to explore, and it might prove difficult to see it all during one visit.

Displays are chronological, starting with the new prehistory gallery that follows the story of Londoners before Roman settlement, progressing to Roman London. The latter is a highlight, with reconstructed rooms and superb sculptures from the Temple

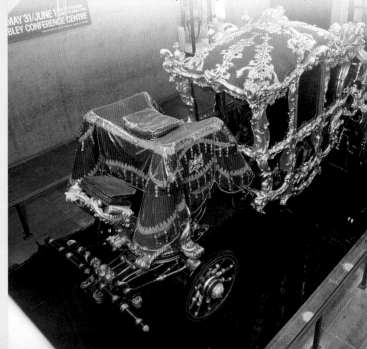

of Mithras discovered close by. Another new exhibition, the Medieval gallery shows objects from recent excavations, never displayed before, shedding light on the Dark Ages of the 15th century and going through more enlightened times up to 1558. Highlights include an audiovisual on the Black Death, a reconstruction of an Anglo-Saxon home and objects from 13th-century Jewish houses in the City of London. In the Stuart section you will find Oliver Cromwell's death mask, the Cheapside (jewellery) Hoard, plague exhibits and the Great Fire Experience, accompanied by a reading from the diary of Samuel Pepys.

Further galleries, from late Stuart times to the present, feature many fascinating large-scale exhibits. Most handsome of all is the opulent Lord Mayor's State Coach, made in 1757. The World City galleries cover the period from the French Revolution to the outbreak of World War I, and in the Victorian Walk section are some fascinating reconstructions of London shop fronts.
www.museumoflondon.org.uk
✚ 132 D3 ✉ London Wall ☎ 0870 444 3851 (recorded info) 🕐 Mon–Sat 10–5:50, Sun 12–5:50. Closed 24–26 Dec, 1 Jan 🖐 Free 🍴 Good café-restaurant (£) Ⓔ Barbican, St Paul's, Moorgate ❓ Family events, including costumed actors, most Sats, Suns and during school hols

ST BARTHOLOMEW THE GREAT
Founded in 1123 by Rahere, the court jester to Henry I, this is London's oldest church. The entrance is an unusual half-timbered Tudor gatehouse, and the atmospheric interior is reminiscent of a small cathedral. It has the best Norman chancel in London (rivalled only by the Chapel of St John in the Tower of London ➤ 37) with Norman piers supporting an upper gallery. There are also some very fine tomb monuments, including that of Rahere.
www.greatstbarts.com
✚ 132 C3 ✉ West Smithfield ☎ 020 7606 5171 🕐 Tue–Fri 8:30–5 (4 in winter), Sat 10:30–1:30, Sun 8:30–1, 2:30–8 🖐 Free 🍴 Le Comptoir Gascon (££), 61 Charterhouse Street Ⓔ Barbican

ST BRIDE'S CHURCH

The Church of St Bride occupies one of the capital's oldest religious sites; during the 6th century St Bridget's Church marked the very first Irish settlement in London. The present church, completed in 1675, is by Christopher Wren, though its interior is modern, having been gutted by a bomb in 1940. The crypt holds an interesting small museum tracing the history of the church and its long connection with the Fleet Street newspaper trade.

www.stbrides.com

✚ 132 E2 ✉ Fleet Street ☎ 020 7427 0133
🕐 Mon–Fri 8–6, Sat 11–3, Sun 10–1, 5–7:30 ✋ Free
🍴 Ye Olde Cheshire Cheese (£) Ⓑ Blackfriars
❓ Lunchtime concerts (most of year, not Lent and Dec)
Tue, Fri 1:15, choral services Sun 11, 6:30

ST KATHARINE DOCKS

To experience London's huge dockland warehouses as they used to be without making the journey east, visit St Katharine

Docks, conveniently close to the Tower of London. Here exotic items such as ostrich feathers, spices, teas, turtles and ivory (up to 22,000 tusks in a year) were once stored. The docks closed in 1968 and were developed to cater for the tourist trade with shops, restaurants and historic sailing ships at anchor. The picturesque late 18th-century Dickens Inn pub-restaurant incorporates 17th-century timbers into its galleried frontage.

✚ 133 F7 ✋ Free 🍴 Dickens Inn (£) Ⓠ Tower Hill

ST PAUL'S CATHEDRAL
Best places to see, pages 32–33.

ST STEPHEN WALBROOK
This is the Lord Mayor of London's parish church and is arguably the finest of all the City's churches. Built by Christopher Wren between 1672 and 1679, its dome was the first in England and was clearly a prototype for Wren's engineering *tour de force*, the dome of St Paul's Cathedral. The church was

beautifully restored between 1978 and 1987, with the original dark-wood fittings making a striking contrast to the gleaming white marble floor and the controversial giant white 'Camembert cheese' stone altarpiece, designed by Sir Henry Moore in 1972.

✚ 132 E4 ✉ 39 Walbrook ☎ 020 7283 4444 🕐 Mon–Thu 10–4, Fri 10–3 ✋ Free 🍴 Sweetings (££), 39 Queen Victoria Street Ⓠ Bank, Cannon Street

SIR JOHN SOANE'S MUSEUM

In terms of size and layout, this extraordinary labyrinthine museum is the most unusual art and antiquities collection in the capital. It was formerly the home of the designer and architect Sir John Soane (1753–1837) and has, according to the terms specified by Soane himself, been kept exactly in its original condition. Much of this magpie collection is arranged around a central court and is aided and abetted by false walls, alcoves, domes and skylights. Its treasures include masterpieces (cleverly hung on hinged panels which go flat to the wall to save space) by Turner, Canaletto and Hogarth (including the famous *Rake's Progress* series), a sarcophagus from the Valley of the Kings, a bizarre Gothic folly entitled the 'Monk's Parlour', plus sculptures and stone fragments galore.

www.soane.org

✚ 131 D8 ✉ 13 Lincoln's Inn Fields ☎ 020 7405 2107 🕐 Tue–Sat 10–5. Also first Tue of month 6–9. Closed all public hols ✋ Free (charge for exhibitions) 🍴 The Lamb (£) Ⓠ Holborn ❓ Guided tour Sat 2:30 (moderate)

TOWER BRIDGE

One of London's best-known landmarks, Tower Bridge was built between 1886 and 1894 and hailed as one of the greatest engineering feats of its day. It is basically a classic Victorian iron and steel structure, clad in stone to match the medieval appearance of its neighbour, the Tower of London. Until quite recently it was the last road bridge across the Thames before the river reaches the North Sea, and it remains London's only drawbridge. This function was to allow large ships to pass into the busy Upper Pool of London, which was a hive of warehouse activity in Victorian times. At its peak, its bascules (drawbridges) were like yo-yos, up and down 50 times a day. Today they open on average around 18 times a week to allow tall ships, cruise ships and naval vessels through.

The structure now houses the **Tower Bridge Exhibition,** an informative multimedia exhibition that explains the history of the bridge. You can also step right into the bowels of the building to see the original Victorian engine rooms which were used to raise the bascules from 1894 to 1976. The high-level walkways, 43m (141ft) above the river, were designed to allow pedestrians to cross when the drawbridges were raised, and the views are unbeatable. Even from ground level Tower Bridge is one of the city's great vantage points.

www.towerbridge.org.uk

✚ 133 F7

Tower Bridge Exhibition

✉ Tower Bridge ☎ 020 7403 3761 🕔 Apr–Sep 10–6:30; Oct–Mar 9:30–6. Last admission 1 hour before closing ✋ Moderate 🍴 Butler's Wharf Chop House (£–££) 🚇 Tower Hill, London Bridge ❓ Bridge lift information line 020 7940 3984 or see website

TOWER OF LONDON
Best places to see, pages 36–37.

Westminster and the South Bank

SOUTHWARK

LAMBETH

WESTMINSTER

This district is dominated by the Thames, an iconic symbol of the city. The river's banks present two contrasting images.

The north bank is lined, in general, with stately buildings connected with money, power and government and includes

the Houses of Parliament and Westminster Abbey. Here are buildings of political, historical and religious significance bringing a sense of stability to the city. The South Bank has a very different flavour. Early theatre thrived here and Shakespeare's reconstructed Globe Theatre is testament to this. After World War II this area of wasteland was given a makeover with the construction of the Royal Festival Hall and the South Bank Centre, continuing the area's connection with the arts. As a new millennium approached further attractions were added, most popular of all being the London Eye. The old Bankside Power Station was transformed into the highly successful Tate Modern, further enhancing the South Bank's cultural status as a magnet for arts buffs.

BRITAIN AT WAR EXPERIENCE

Sheltered deep beneath the arches of London Bridge, this is an evocative museum showing what it was like to live in the capital during World War II, and particularly during the Blitz of 1940–41. Aside from examining a huge number of well-displayed original period objects, you can sit in an air-raid shelter or walk through an eerily authentic bombed-out building. Older visitors will enjoy the bittersweet nostalgia of such displays as life on the Home Front, evacuation, movie news and re-created shopfronts, while younger ones will enjoy the drama without experiencing the trauma of those momentous years.

www.britainatwar.co.uk

✚ 139 A5 ✉ 64–66 Tooley Street ☎ 020 7403 3171 🕔 Daily 10–6 (Oct–Mar till 5) (last admission 1 hour before closing) ✋ Expensive
🍴 Butler's Wharf Chop House (£–££) 🚇 London Bridge

CLINK PRISON MUSEUM

From the early 16th century until 1780, the Clink, 'a very dismal hole', was the jail of the Bishops of Winchester, used to incarcerate the lowlife of Bankside – including prostitutes, drunks, debtors, and actors who had 'broken the peace'. In fact it was so notorious that it entered the English language as a synonym for jail. Not that the bishop held the moral high ground. He acted effectively as protection racketeer and pimp, licensing, and profiting from, the various illegal activities that went on in the badlands of Bankside. You can learn all about these times at the Clink Prison Museum. Alongside, part of a wall with a great rose window is all that survives of the Bishop's Palace, Winchester House, built in 1109.

www.clinkprison.co.uk

✚ 132 F4 ✉ 1 Clink Street ☎ 020 7403 0900 ⏱ Mon–Fri 10–6, Sat, Sun 10–9 ✋ Moderate 🍴 fish!, Cathedral Street, Borough Market (££) 🚇 London Bridge (10-min walk)

DESIGN MUSEUM

This was set up in 1989 as the brainchild of Britain's leading design and style guru, Sir Terence Conran, to promote an awareness of the importance of design and the contribution it makes to everyday life, particularly when related to mass-produced objects. Although this may not sound particularly promising (and the severe lines of its brilliant white Bauhaus building hardly provide

reassurance to the casual visitor), it is well worth a visit. The collection divides broadly into two parts. The more conventional historic part shows the design evolution of familiar workaday items, such as domestic appliances, cameras and cars. The upper Review Gallery is an intriguing showcase for the very latest ideas; some currently in production, some at prototype stage, others stuck permanently on the drawing board. Interactive computer stations cater for a new generation of would-be designers.

www.designmuseum.org

✚ 139 A7 ✉ 28 Shad Thames ☎ 0870 833 9955; 0870 909 9009 ⏱ Daily 10–5:45 (Fri 10–9). Closed 25–26 Dec (last admission 5:15) ✋ Expensive 🍴 Blueprint Café restaurant (££), café (£) 🚇 London Bridge, Tower Hill

HMS *BELFAST*

HMS *Belfast* is Europe's last surviving big warship from World War II and occupies a spectacular permanent mooring site on the Thames just upstream from Tower Bridge. Launched in 1938, she saw action in the Arctic, at the D-Day Normandy landings and in the Korean War from 1950 to 1952.

Today her seven decks, which once accommodated a crew of up to 800 men, serve as a museum, giving landlubbers a salty flavour of the rigours of serving at sea. The bridge, galley, operations room, punishment cells, engine and boiler rooms can all be explored. There are also various naval displays. Check out the exhibition Life at Sea.

www.iwm.org.uk

✚ 133 F6 ✉ Morgan's Lane, off Tooley Street ☎ 020 7940 6300 ⊘ Daily Mar–Oct 10–6; Nov–Feb 10–5. Closed 24–26 Dec (last admission 45 mins before closing) ♿ Expensive; children free 🍴 Café (£) 🚇 London Bridge, Tower Hill. Ferry from Tower Hill pier in summer

HOUSES OF PARLIAMENT

Best places to see, pages 26–27.

IMPERIAL WAR MUSEUM

Dedicated to an account of world conflict during the 20th century, the Imperial War Museum has the most impressive entrance of any London museum. Suspended from the ceiling of its glass atrium and occupying two floors around the atrium are World War II fighter planes, biplanes from the Great War, a V2 rocket, a Polaris

missile, field guns, tanks, submarines, plus over 40 other large exhibits. This is a thought-provoking museum, telling the story of war dispassionately, often from the point of view of the ordinary soldier or the folks left at home. The emphasis is on the two World Wars. Each has a large walk-in section where you can experience the horrors of the trenches or the claustrophobia of an air-raid shelter, then the aftermath of a bombing raid. Most harrowing is the The Holocaust exhibition, not considered suitable for young children.

The narrative collection is brilliantly chosen, containing many personal and everyday objects from the trenches, the concentration camps, the Far East, the Eastern Front, the Atlantic Ocean and all the significant theatres of war. These are combined with memorabilia such as recruiting posters, dramatic contemporary film footage and spoken first-hand accounts from ordinary combatants and survivors.

Conflicts since 1945 are also well handled and the Secret War Exhibition, detailing clandestine operations from World War I to the present day, is fascinating. The top floor features the gallery, Crimes Against Humanity, considered suitable for under 16s.

www.iwm.org.uk

✚ 138 C2 ✉ Lambeth Road ☎ 020 7416 5320 (recorded) 🕓 Daily 10–6. Closed 24–26 Dec ♿ Free 🍴 Café (£) Ⓜ Lambeth North, Elephant & Castle, Waterloo

JEWEL TOWER

This solitary tower is one of the few remaining parts of the old Palace of Westminster (➤ 27). Built in 1366, it was used to house the personal valuables of Edward III and was known as the Royal Wardrobe. Today it makes an excellent introduction to the Houses of Parliament with an exhibition about their history and procedural practices. You can also take a 'tour' of Parliament on a multimedia touch-screen machine.

www.english-heritage.org.uk

✚ 137 C6 ⊠ Old Palace Yard, Abingdon Street ☎ 020 7222 2219 ⓒ Apr–Oct daily 10–5; Nov–Mar daily 10–4 👋 Inexpensive ⅋ The Cinnamon Club (££), Great Smith Street ☎ 020 7222 2555 ⓒ Westminster, St James's Park

LONDON AQUARIUM

This is the capital's first real aquarium and one of the new generation of maximum-visibility, large-tank, natural-atmosphere aquaria that are currently enjoying great popularity. Giant tanks, 8m (26ft) high, feature Atlantic and Pacific displays. The latter is home to sand tiger and brown sharks, and large rays that glide silently between giant, sunken replicas of Easter Island statues. The Reef and Living Coral exhibit and the Indian Ocean tank is where you can watch the sharks and piranhas feed or listen to rainforest talks, while the highlight for many children is the chance to stroke a ray in the touch pool.

www.londonaquarium.co.uk

✚ 137 B7 ⊠ County Hall, Riverside Building, Westminster Bridge Road ☎ 020 7967 8000 ⓒ Daily 10–6 (last admission 5) 👋 Expensive ⅋ Options in County Hall and near by ⓒ Waterloo, Westminster

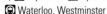

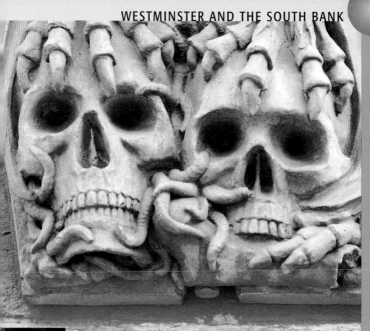

LONDON DUNGEON

'Abandon hope all who enter here' is the message of the London Dungeon, the world's first and foremost museum of medieval (and other) horrors. It was begun in 1975 by a London housewife whose children were disappointed by the lack of blood and gore on display at the Tower of London. Certainly no one leaves the Dungeon with such complaints! The dark tunnels beneath London Bridge now include many more blood-curdling special effects, with a 'dark ride' (in every sense) and costumed actors to enhance the scream factor. Ghouls and the curious, including most of London's overseas teenagers, make this one of the capital's most visited attractions, but this is definitely not a place for young children or the faint of heart.

www.thedungeons.com

✚ 139 A5 ✉ Tooley Street ☎ 020 7403 7221 (general enquiries)
🕐 Daily 10–5:30 (last admission). Closed 25 Dec ✋ Very expensive
🍴 Butler's Wharf Chop House (£–££) 🚇 London Bridge

LONDON EYE

This giant landmark wheel was erected as part of the capital's Millennium celebrations and has quickly become one of the hottest attraction tickets in town. Its 32 observation capsules soar majestically 135m (443ft) directly above the Thames, making it the tallest wheel of its kind in the world. A full revolution takes 30 minutes, offering magnificent views right across the heart of central London and far beyond.

A limited number of seats is available to those who show up in person (these are quickly snapped up); the rest are reserved by telephone. The best advice is to reserve well ahead. Even with a ticket, however, boarding takes around 30 minutes.

www.ba-londoneye.com

✚ 137 A7 ✉ Riverside Gardens, next to County Hall ☎ 0870 990 8881; booking 0870 500 0600 🕐 Jun–Sep daily 10–9; Oct–May daily 10–8 ✋ Expensive ✋ Riverfront cafés 🚇 Waterloo

OXO TOWER

Built in 1930 for the Oxo company, this splendid art deco tower has long been a Thames landmark, but had fallen into such disrepair that demolition was likely. Now lovingly restored, its huge illuminated red O X O trademark letters make it one of the most striking sights on the London night skyline. The tower houses exhibition spaces, eating places (open daily), award-winning craft and designer shops and studios (closed Monday). There are panoramic views from the free 8th-floor public viewing gallery.

www.oxotower.co.uk

✚ 132 F2 ✉ Oxo Tower Wharf, Barge House Street, South Bank ☎ 020 7401 2255 🕐 Viewing gallery 11–10 ✋ Free 🚇 Blackfriars, Waterloo

SHAKESPEARE'S GLOBE

In May 1997 Shakespeare's circular wooden Globe Theatre was completed after 25 years' hard work, the dream of American film and theatre director, the late Sam Wanamaker. Constructed according to late 16th-century techniques, it was the first thatched building to be erected in London since the Great Fire of 1666. The Globe Exhibition, telling the story behind this remarkable project, features a major exhibition on the world of Shakespeare and includes a theatrical tour.

www.shakespeares-globe.org

✚ 132 F3 ✉ 21 New Globe Walk, Bankside
☎ 020 7902 1400 ⏰ Mid-Apr to mid-Oct
Mon–Sat 9–12, 12:30–5, Sun 9–11:30, 12–5; mid-Oct to mid-Apr daily 10–5. Closed 24, 25 Dec
🍴 Globe Café (£), Globe Restaurant (££)
🚇 Mansion House, Southwark 💷 Expensive
❓ Guided tours. Performances May–Oct ☎ 020 7401 9919

SOUTHWARK CATHEDRAL

Often overlooked by visitors, Southwark Cathedral boasts one of the oldest and most interesting church interiors in the capital. Construction began in 1220 and was finished some 200 years later (though most of its exterior features were remodelled much later). The nave retains some original stonework and fascinating 15th-century ornamental carvings – one depicts the devil swallowing Judas Iscariot. There are several grand monuments, the most notable being to the area's most famous parishioner, William Shakespeare, who lived in Southwark from 1599 to 1611. His brother Edmund (died 1607) and other fellow dramatists are buried in the cathedral.

www.dswark.org/cathedral

✚ 138 A4 ✉ Cathedral Street ☎ 020 7367 6700 🕐 Mon–Fri 7:30–6, Sat, Sun 8:30–6 ♿ Moderate 🍴 Café/restaurant (£) in refectory 🚇 London Bridge

TATE BRITAIN AND TATE MODERN

In 2000, the Tate Gallery split into two – Tate Britain and Tate Modern.

Tate Britain occupies the original Millbank site and retains its function as the showcase of British art from 1500 to the present. The national collection now fills Henry Tate's refurbished building. It is impossible to say what will be on display as exhibits go in and out of storage and are also rotated to provincial Tate museums. However the highlight of the British collection is the Turner Bequest, with many of the finest works of J M W Turner, regarded by many as Britain's greatest landscape painter. Tate Britain has a superb collection of High Victorian and Pre-Raphaelite pictures and the controversial Turner Prize is staged annually here.

Tate Modern, housed in Sir Giles Gilbert Scott's formidable Bankside Power Station, on the South Bank of the Thames opposite St Paul's, opened in summer 2000. It was not only the first major new museum in the capital for over a century but also one of the most important contemporary galleries in the world, devoted to art post-1900. Look for works by Picasso, Matisse, Mondrian, Duchamp, Bacon, Rothko and Warhol.

www.tate.org.uk

Tate Britain

➕ 137 D6 ✉ Millbank ☎ 020 7887 8000; recorded info 020 7887 8008
🕐 Daily 10–5:50 (also first Fri in month 6pm–10pm). Closed 24–26 Dec
💷 Free (charge for exhibitions) 🍴 Tate Café (£); Rex Whistler Restaurant
(£££) ☎ 020 7887 8825 🚇 Westminster, Vauxhall ❓ Free guided tours daily.
Multimedia guides (inexpensive). Art Trolley activities for children (aged 5+)
Sun 2–5. Shuttle service by boat to Tate Modern

Tate Modern

➕ 132 F3 ✉ Bankside ☎ As above 🕐 Sun–Thu 10–6, Fri, Sat 10–10 (last
admission 45 mins before closing) 💷 Free 🍴 Tate Modern Restaurant (£££)
🚇 Southwark ❓ Daily guided tours (free). Multimedia guides (inexpensive).
Footbridge from St Paul's Cathedral. Shuttle service by boat to Tate Britain

The Unilever Series:
Juan Muñoz

WESTMINSTER ABBEY
Best places to see, pages 40–41.

WESTMINSTER CATHEDRAL
Not to be confused with the more illustrious abbey of the same name, Westminster Cathedral is London's principal Roman Catholic church. Its foundation is relatively modern: it was built between 1896 and 1903. The Byzantine campanile (accessible by elevator) is one of the capital's lesser-known landmarks, towering some 83m (272ft) high and offering great views over central London. The cathedral interior is famous for some of the finest and most varied marble-work in the country, though it has never been completed and much of the huge nave ceiling still shows bare brickwork.

www.westminstercathedral.org.uk

✚ 136 C4 ✉ Victoria Street ☎ 020 7798 9055 🕓 Mon–Fri 7–7, Sat, Sun 8–7. Tower Apr–Nov daily 9:30–12:30, 1–5; Dec–Mar Thu–Sun 9–5 ✋ Cathedral free (donations appreciated); tower moderate 🚇 Victoria

Knightsbridge, Kensington and Chelsea

Once remote from the City of London, these premier residential districts and former villages were favoured for their healthy air well away from the dirt and pollution of early London.

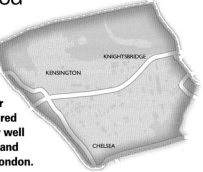

Today they retain their exclusivity with their grand Georgian houses and leafy squares that have attracted the wealthy and have become home to several embassies and consulates. Kensington gained its fashionable reputation in the late 17th century when the royalty moved to Kensington Palace. Popular with sightseers and shoppers, the district leads into South Kensington, where there are museums containing some of the best collections of arts and crafts, science and natural history in the world. Next is Knightsbridge, an even more exclusive address, whose affluent residents use the world-famous Harrods department store as their local shop. Most visitors are happy just to gaze at the richness and variety of the stock, the lavish interiors and tempting food halls. To the south is the more bohemian Chelsea. Still a classy and incredibly expensive district in which to live, it is now synonymous with 'Swinging London' and popular for shopping in the lively King's Road.

APSLEY HOUSE

Apsley House, also known as the Wellington Museum, was the London home of Arthur Wellesley, first Duke of Wellington, from 1829 until his death in 1852. Wellington was the greatest soldier of his day, achieving major military successes in India, Spain and Portugal before crowning his career with the defeat of Napoleon at Waterloo in 1815.

The museum is divided into two parts. Collections of plates and china, magnificent table centrepieces, swords, medals and so on relate to the Duke's adventures, and there is also an outstanding picture collection with works by many famous old masters. Intriguingly, the most memorable piece is a heroic oversized statue of Napoleon by Canova (commissioned by the Little Emperor himself) in which he is depicted as a god.

www.english-heritage.org.uk

✚ 136 A2 ✉ 149 Piccadilly, Hyde Park Corner ☎ 020 7499 5676 🕐 Apr–Oct Tue–Sun 10–5 (last admission 4:30); Nov–Mar 10–4. Closed Mon (open public hol Mon 10–5, except May Day), 24–26 Dec, 1 Jan ✋ Moderate 🍽 The Grenadier (£) 🚇 Hyde Park Corner

CHELSEA

One of London's most fashionable suburbs in every sense, Chelsea was synonymous with both London's 'Swinging 60s' and the late 1970s punk rock movement. The latter was in fact born here, just off the famous King's

Road. Today it is more classy though still very lively and is best explored on foot (➤ 92–93).

✛ 135 F6

HARRODS

Harrods is much more than just a shop: it is an internationally famous institution and even the most reluctant shopper should venture into its cathedral-like portals. The store began trading here in 1849 as a small, family-run grocery shop and by 1911 the present magnificent terracotta building was complete. Occupying over 10ha (25 acres), it is Britain's biggest department store.

Among the highlights are the stylish Food Halls. The Meat Hall is gloriously decorated with 1902 tiles, while the fresh-fish display is an extravaganza of the bounty of the sea.

www.harrods.com

✛ 135 B8 ✉ 87–135 Brompton Road ☎ 020 7730 1234 🕐 Mon–Sat 10–8, Sun 12–6 🍴 Variety in store (£–£££) 🚇 Knightsbridge ❓ No one admitted wearing scruffy clothes, tank tops (men), short shorts or cycling shorts. Backpacks to be left in lockers. Charge for toilets

a walk around Chelsea

Start from Sloane Square underground station and walk straight ahead, down the King's Road, with Sloane Square and its statue of Sir Hans Sloane on your right.

About 100m (110yds) past the square turn left into Cheltenham Terrace with the Duke of York's (Territorial Army) Headquarters to your left. Turn right into St Leonard's Terrace, former home of Bram Stoker (the creator of Dracula), with the green fields of Burtons Court to your left.

The building on the other side of the fields is the Royal Hospital, home to the famous Chelsea pensioners.

Turn left into Smith Street, then right into Royal Hospital Road (or left to visit the Hospital), passing the National Army Museum (➤ 96–97). Turn left into Tite Street, which includes such famous former residents as Oscar Wilde (No 34), John Singer Sargent (No 31) and Augustus John

(No 33). Turn right onto Dilke Street, with a glimpse through the side gate of the Chelsea Physic Garden.

Physic simply means 'of things natural'. This is the second-oldest botanic garden in the country, founded in 1673.

Turn left into Swan Walk past the Physic Garden entrance, then right onto Chelsea Embankment, with Cheyne Walk a short way on to your right.

This handsome terrace was also home to some of Chelsea's famous artists and writers including George Eliot (No 4) and Dante Gabrielle Rossetti (No 16).

Continue along the Embankment, past pretty pink Albert Bridge, to Chelsea Old Church.

A statue of Sir Thomas More sits outside the church and his intended tomb, inside, is occupied by his wife.

Turn right into Church Street until you rejoin the shops of King's Road, then turn right to return to Sloane Square.

Distance 5–6km (3–3.75 miles)
Time 2–6 hours depending on visits
Start/end point 🚇 Sloane Square ✚ 136 D2
Lunch Pizza Express (£) ✉ 152 King's Road ☎ 020 7351 5031

Royal Hospital, Chelsea ☎ 020 7881 5200
🕐 Daily 10–12, 2–4. Closed Sun Oct–Mar 👛 Free, donations welcome

Chelsea Physic Garden ☎ 020 7352 5646 🕐 Apr–Oct Wed 12–5, Sun 2–6 👛 Moderate

HYDE PARK

The largest and most famous of central London's open spaces, Hyde Park covers 138ha (340 acres) and was once the royal hunting ground of Henry VIII and Elizabeth I.

At its northeast corner, at the very end of Oxford Street, is Marble Arch; it was originally erected in front of Buckingham Palace but was moved as a result of palace redevelopment. Nearby is Speakers' Corner, London's most famous 'soapbox' where anyone may air their views (within reason).

Flowing through the park is the Serpentine lake, created in 1730, and just west of here is the **Serpentine Gallery,** featuring revolving exhibitions of contemporary art. On the other side of the lake is the unusual and controversial Princess Diana Memorial Fountain, which was opened in 2004 by the Queen.

www.royalparks.gov.uk

➕ 129 F8 ☎ 020 7298 2100 (Park Office) 🕐 Daily 5am–midnight 💂 Free
Ⓜ Marble Arch, Knightsbridge, Hyde Park Corner

Serpentine Gallery

☎ 020 7298 1501; www.serpentinegallery.org 🕐 Daily 10–6 during exhibitions 💂 Free Ⓜ Lancaster Gate, South Kensington

KENSINGTON PALACE AND GARDENS

William III was the first monarch to set up home in Kensington Palace, in 1689, and it was here in 1819 that the future Queen Victoria was born. Royal patronage continues with several members of the present royal family having palace apartments. In September 1997 it was a focus of the country's grief as the last home of the late Princess Diana, when thousands of floral tributes were piled up in front of the palace gates. There is no memorial within the palace to Diana but a memorial playground is close by in Kensington Gardens.

The fabric of the present palace, which actually resembles a country house in both style and size, dates largely from the early 18th century. The parts that are open to the visitor divide broadly into two areas: the State Apartments and the Royal Ceremonial Dress Collection. The Apartments are striking for their magnificent ceiling paintings by William Kent and some impressive and curious *trompe-l'œil* effects. The Royal Ceremonial Dress Collection has a superb collection of court finery. Surrounding the palace are pretty sunken gardens and an orangery, now a restaurant.

Outside the palace gates is Kensington Gardens, which runs east into Hyde Park. This pretty lawned expanse boasts two famous statues. To the north is Peter Pan, and to the south, near the Royal Albert Hall, is the amazingly intricate 53m-high (174ft) Albert Memorial, which is dedicated to Prince Albert, Queen Victoria's much-loved consort.

www.hrp.org.uk

✚ 134 A4, 129 F5 ✉ Kensington Gardens ☎ 020 7937 9561; 0870 751 5176 (info line) 🕐 Daily Mar–Oct 10–6 (last admission 5); Nov–Feb 10–5 (last admission 4). Closed 24–26 Dec 💷 Expensive 🍴 The Orangery (£–££) 🚇 High Street Kensington, Queensway ❓ Audioguide included in ticket price

LEIGHTON HOUSE

The distinguished Victorian artist Frederic Lord Leighton (1830–96) created this beautiful romantic house between 1864 and 1866 and lived here until his death in 1896. The centrepiece is the Arab Hall, a glorious mini-Alhambra featuring a dome from Damascus, window screens from Cairo and Leighton's highly valued, rare collection of 15th- and 16th-century Islamic tiles from Cairo, Damascus and Rhodes. The other rooms are much more restrained but contain some fine works by Lord Leighton and his famous Pre-Raphaelite associates.

www.rbkc.gov.uk

🚩 134 C2 ✉ 12 Holland Park Road ☎ 020 7602 3316
🕐 Wed–Mon 11–5:30. Closed 25–26 Dec, 1 Jan 🚶 Moderate 🍴 Several on High Street Kensington (£–££)
🚇 High Street Kensington

NATIONAL ARMY MUSEUM

The first professional British Army was formed in 1485 and this museum, refurbished and upgraded, covers its history in the five centuries to date. Audiovisual presentations, dioramas and lifelike soldier mannequins bring to life the lot of the ordinary soldier in a manner that concentrates more on the daily hardships than on the glory of war.

Start in the basement with Redcoats, which moves from Agincourt to the American War of Independence. As well as admiring the fine display of swords you can try on a civil war helmet and feel the weight of a cannon shot.

The Road to Waterloo follows the story of the soldiers in Wellington's army and includes a huge, scale model of the battlefield (at the critical moment of 7.15pm on 18 June, 1815) and the skeleton of Napoleon's beloved war horse, Marengo. Move on briskly through the Victorian Soldier exhibitions noting Florence Nightingale's lamp, quite unlike the lantern of popular imagination. The Brixmis exhibition on information gathered during the Cold War is also surprisingly interesting.

Displays on the two World Wars and the modern British Army (1965 to date) bring the story up to date, though if you are particularly interested in this period you would be better off paying a visit to the Imperial War Museum (➤ 79).

www.national-army-museum.ac.uk

🕂 136 F1 ✉ Royal Hospital Road, Chelsea ☎ 020 7730 0717; 020 7881 2455 (info line) 🕐 Daily 10–5:30. Closed 24–26 Dec, 1 Jan, Good Fri, May Day 💷 Free 🍴 Café (£) 🚇 Sloane Square, then 10 minutes' walk along King's Road into Smith Street ❓ Self-guiding tours available

NATURAL HISTORY MUSEUM
Best places to see, pages 30–31.

SCIENCE MUSEUM
Best places to see, pages 34–35.

VICTORIA AND ALBERT MUSEUM
Best places to see, pages 38–39.

Outer London

When the crowds and noise of central London begin to make you wonder if you made the right choice by taking a city holiday, it's time to head out of town. Fortunately you don't have to go far before the whole atmosphere changes.

The easiest and most popular excursion is downriver to Greenwich, full of history, good shopping and restaurants. Upriver lie Hampton Court Palace and the Royal Botanic Gardens at Kew. Each makes a glorious sunny summer's day out, but don't try to combine the two – there is far too much to see. Return visitors to London should seek out the low-key but highly enjoyable pleasures of riverside Richmond, and Twickenham, on the opposite side of the Thames.

GREENWICH

Greenwich is some 10km (6 miles) east of the centre of London, accessed by train from London Bridge or on the Dockland Light Railway (DLR) direct. Or take a boat to arrive the traditional way, or perhaps the DLR to Island Gardens, directly opposite Greenwich. From here you can enjoy a river view that has changed little in centuries, then simply walk under the Thames via the Greenwich Foot Tunnel. Though suffering from heavy traffic and summer crowds, Greenwich retains something of a village atmosphere with lots of interesting small shops, a thriving market, an abundance of historic attractions and one of London's finest parks.

www.greenwich.gov.uk; www.nmm.ac.uk

✚ 140 E2 🛈 2 Cutty Sark Gardens ☎ 0870 608 2000 🕔 Daily 10–5
❓ Guided walking tours depart daily 12:15, 2:15 ☎ 020 8858 6169

National Maritime Museum

The National Maritime Museum was given a major makeover to celebrate the Millennium and while it may be the world's largest and most important maritime museum, it is appealing to even the most confirmed land lubber.

At its heart is the Neptune Court, a dramatic glassed-over courtyard with the museum's largest objects, such as the carved and gilded state barge made for Frederick, Prince of Wales, in 1732. Near here are 15 or so major galleries that explain the history and role of maritime Greenwich, Britain as a once-great sea power and more worldwide topics such ocean exploration. Some of the finest ship models and great maritime paintings are also here. Younger visitors should head for All Hands and The Bridge, two hands-on galleries.

✉ Greenwich Park ☎ 020 8312 6565 (recorded info); 020 8858 4422 (switchboard) 🕔 Sep–Jun daily 10–5, Jul–Aug daily 10–6 (last admission 30 mins before closing). Closed 24–26 Dec 💷 Free 🍽 The Regatta Café (£)
🚈 DLR to Cutty Sark 🚉 Greenwich from London Bridge ⛴ Greenwich Pier

Royal Observatory

The Royal Observatory was founded in 1675 by Charles II to find out the 'so-much desired longitude of places for perfecting the art

of (sea) navigation'. High on a mound in Greenwich Park, and commanding a splendid view, it was designed by Sir Christopher Wren and functioned as Britain's principal observatory until 1945. Today it is a museum that tells the history of the observatory and offers a crash course in the measurement of time and astronomy. Displays are well explained and feature some beautiful historical instruments. There is also a fascinating camera obscura. The prime attraction for most visitors, however, is to be photographed standing astride the 0° longitude line (which passes right through the observatory) with one foot in the eastern hemisphere and one foot in the western.

✉ Greenwich Park ☎ See National Maritime Museum opposite 🕐 Sep–Jun daily 10–5, Jul–Aug daily 10–6. Closed 24–26 Dec 👎 Free 🍴 The Regatta Café (£), National Maritime Museum (➤ opposite) 🚇 DLR to Cutty Sark 🚆 Greenwich from London Bridge 🚢 River boat to Greenwich Pier

Queen's House

This exquisite miniature palace is set at the heart of Greenwich's historic riverfront complex and was the very first classical-style building in England, begun in 1616. It was designed by Inigo Jones. The queen in question was originally Anne of Denmark, wife of James I, though by the time of completion in 1635 she had died and Henrietta Maria, wife of Charles I, assumed tenancy.

✉ Greenwich Park ☎ See National Maritime Museum opposite 🕐 Sep–Jun daily 10–5; Jul–Aug daily 10–6. Closed 24–26 Dec 👎 Free 🍴 The Regatta Café (£), National Maritime Museum (➤ opposite) 🚇 DLR to Cutty Sark 🚆 Greenwich from London Bridge 🚢 Greenwich Pier

a walk around Greenwich

The maritime heritage of Greenwich is immediately apparent even before you land at Greenwich Pier, where tall masts and rigging signal the **Cutty Sark.** Launched in 1869, this is the last surviving British sailing clipper designed to carry cargoes between Britain and the Orient. In 1871 she broke the world record for sailings between London and China, completing the trip in 107 days, and she is famous for her collection of ships' figureheads.

Pick up a map from the tourist office in Cutty Sark Gardens then walk up Greenwich Church Street and go through the market to emerge on King William Walk. Turn right and enter Greenwich Park.

Follow any of the paths that lead up to the Royal Observatory (▶ 101), from where you can enjoy one of London's finest views.

Continue along Blackheath Avenue.

Turn left towards the bandstand, the lovely park gardens and the adjacent wilderness area, where deer have lived for centuries.

Walk back downhill and exit the park near the boating pond into Park Row, then turn left into Romney Road to the entrance to the Old Royal Naval College and Chapel.

This majestic baroque complex was built by Sir Christopher Wren between 1694 and 1745 as a home for Royal Naval Pensioners. They left in 1869 and until recently the building was used as a Royal Naval College.

Distance Approximately 3km (2 miles)
Time 2–4 hours, depending on visits
Start point Greenwich Pier ✚ 140 E2
⊕ DLR to Island Gardens, then foot tunnel
⊕ Greenwich from London Bridge
⊟ River boat to Greenwich Pier
End point Old Royal Naval College (next to Greenwich Pier)
Lunch Picnic in the park

Cutty Sark ☎ 020 8858 3445 ⊙ Currently closed for refurbishment. Phone for information

Old Royal Naval College and Chapel
✚ 140 E2 ☎ 020 8269 4747;
www.oldroyalnavalcollege.org ⊙ Daily 10–5
⊙ Free

HAMPSTEAD

Leafy Hampstead, London's most famous 'village', was developed as a spa in the 18th century and became a fashionable and exclusive retreat favoured by many prominent writers and artists. Spotting name plaques among the many beautiful former homes of luminaries such as Lord Byron, John Keats, H G Wells, Robert Louis Stephenson, D H Lawrence, John Constable and the like is a favourite visitor pastime. The steep narrow streets around the centre are very well preserved and retain an intimate feel. The most appealing include Flask Walk, Well Walk (where you'll find the original spa fountain), Holly Walk, Hampstead Grove and Church Row. Meanwhile, Hampstead High Street and Heath Street bristle with trendy restaurants, cafés and a good variety of small independent shops that cater to the well-heeled residents.

There are a number of low-key sights in the centre. **Burgh House** acts as a local museum; **Fenton House,** built in 1693, holds ceramics and a renowned collection of historic keyboard instruments; **Keats' House,** where the poet John Keats lived for almost two years, is a delightful spot, where *Ode to a Nightingale* and many other fine poems were written. Just south of here is the **Freud Museum,** where Sigmund Freud lived from 1938 until his death in 1939.

Hampstead's other claim to fame is Hampstead Heath, London's largest and most famous heathland, covering some 324ha (800 acres). The heath is one of north London's favourite

summer walking spots and its ponds are also used for swimming. Parliament Hill is a traditional Sunday venue for kite-flying and offers great views across to central London. Much of the heath consists of undeveloped woodland, the main exception being the landscaped grounds of Kenwood House (➤ 108–109).

✚ 140 C1 🚇 Hampstead

Burgh House

✉ New End Square ☎ 020 7431 0144; www.burghhouse.org.uk
🕐 Wed–Sun 12–5 ✋ Free

Fenton House

✉ Windmill Hill ☎ 020 7435 3471; www.nationaltrust.org.uk 🕐 23 Mar–30 Oct Wed–Fri 2–5, Sat, Sun and public hols 11–5; 5–20 Mar Sat, Sun 2–5
✋ Moderate

Keats' House

✉ Keats Grove ☎ 020 7435 2062 🕐 Tue–Sun 1–5 (closed until late summer 2008) ✋ Moderate

Freud Museum

✉ 20 Maresfield Gardens ☎ 020 7435 2002; www.freud.org.uk
🕐 Wed–Sun 12–5 🚇 Finchley Road ✋ Moderate

HAMPTON COURT PALACE

Work on Hampton Court Palace began in 1514 under the tenure of Henry VIII's Lord Chancellor, Cardinal Wolsey. By 1528, however, Wolsey had fallen from favour and Henry had acquired it for himself. He built it up to be the most lavish palace in England where he fêted European royalty and spent five of his six honeymoons. William III and Mary II commissioned Sir Christopher Wren to remodel the apartments and to give the palace much of its present-day appearance. George II was the last monarch to use Hampton Court.

For most visitors the surviving Tudor pieces are still the palace highlights: the great gatehouse and a magnificent astronomical clock, the capacious Tudor Kitchens stocked with contemporary foods and utensils, and fires ablaze all year round, the sumptuous centrepiece Great Hall and the Chapel Royal with its breathtaking ceiling. The King's Apartments (built by William III) are among the finest baroque state apartments in the world and the Wolsey Rooms hold a fine Renaissance picture gallery, though the palace's greatest artwork, *Triumphs of Caesar* by Mantegna, is in the orangery. The gardens, planted in the late 17th century, are glorious and include the ever-popular maze, the Great Vine

(England's largest) and the Royal Tennis Court. The latter was built in 1626 and real tennis (a hybrid of squash and lawn tennis) is still played here regularly.

www.hrp.org.uk

✚ 140 B4 ✉ Hampton Court, East Mosley ☎ 0870 752 7777 (recorded info on palace); 0870 950 4499 (recorded info on gardens) 🕐 Palace and Maze: end Mar–Oct daily 10–6; Nov–end Mar daily 10–4:30 (last admission 1 hour before closing). Formal Gardens: summer daily 10–7; winter daily 10–5:30. Informal Gardens: summer daily 7am–8pm; winter daily 7–6. Home Park: May–Jul daily 7am–9pm; Apr, Aug, Sep daily 7am–8pm; Mar, Oct daily 7–6; Nov–Feb daily 7–5:30 ✋ All-inclusive ticket to palace and gardens expensive. Maze only moderate. Gardens moderate 🍴 Garden café (£) and restaurant (££) 🚊 Train from Waterloo direct to Hampton Court. Boat from Westminster, Richmond or Kew (summer only) 🚌 111, 216, 411, 416, 451, 461, 513, 726, R68

HIGHGATE

The charming village of Highgate lies just east of Hampstead Heath and like its famous neighbour, Hampstead (▶ 104–105), was a favourite retreat for the upper classes and literary figures, including Samuel Taylor Coleridge (author of *The Rime of the Ancient Mariner*).

Its most popular visitor highlight is Highgate Cemetery. Opened in 1839, the cemetery soon became the fashionable final resting place of politicians, poets, actors and other Victorian personalities. Monuments grew ever larger and more ornate and the cemetery turned into a tourist attraction. The West Cemetery is the real draw, piled high with crumbling catacombs, Egyptian columns and obelisks, ivy-clad vaults and grand mausoleums. It looks like the set for a horror movie and is said to have inspired Bram Stoker (the author of *Dracula*). However, the most famous personalities are buried in the East Cemetery and include Karl Marx, Sir Ralph Richardson, Mary Ann Evans (pen-name George Eliot) and comedian Max Wall.

www.highgate-cemetery.org

✚ 140 C1 ✉ Swain's Lane ☎ 020 8340 1834 🕓 East Cemetery Mon–Fri 10–4:30 (3:30 winter), Sat, Sun 11–4:30 (3:30 winter). West Cemetery, admission by tour only; Sat–Sun 11–4 each hour, Mon–Fri tours at 2 (advisable to book). Nov–Mar tours at weekends only 11–3 ✋ East Cemetery inexpensive; West Cemetery moderate for tours 🚇 Highgate/Archway ❓ No children under 8 in the West Cemetery

KENWOOD HOUSE

If you would like to see a real country house without straying too far then visit Kenwood, on the north of Hampstead Heath (▶ 104–105). Built in 1616, it was

remodelled in 1764 by Robert Adam, whose signature pale blue, neo-classical design is apparent as soon as you enter the house. The paintings at Kenwood are known as the Iveagh Bequest and form one of the most important collections bequeathed to the nation. They are mostly 17th- and 18th-century works from the English, Dutch and French schools, though recent additions include much earlier paintings by Botticelli and Hans Memling. The most famous is a Rembrandt self-portrait, acknowledged as one of his very best. Also notable are works by Frans Hals and Vermeer. New acquisitions include Constable's *Hampstead Heath with Pond and Bathers*. The architectural *tour de force* of the house is the library, with its elaborately decorated tunnel-vaulted ceiling and Corinthian columns. It is considered one of Adam's finest interiors.

The beautiful gardens are the most cultivated part of Hampstead Heath, with a grassed amphitheatre sloping down to a lake. During summer this becomes London's finest outdoor classical music venue – American visitors note, Handel's *Fireworks Music* is played every 4 July with accompanying pyrotechnics!

www.english-heritage.org.uk

➕ 140 C1 ✉ Hampstead Lane ☎ 020 8348 1286 🕐 Apr–Oct daily 11–5; Nov–Mar daily 11–4. Closed 24–25 Dec, 1 Jan ✋ Free (charge for exhibitions) 🍴 Restaurant, café (£–££) Ⓜ Hampstead, then bus 210

KEW, ROYAL BOTANIC GARDENS

Founded in the late 18th century, Kew Gardens, a huge park of almost 122ha (300 acres), holds a marvellous collection of plants, trees and flowers from every corner of the globe. Most of the species are grown outdoors, but huge glass and wrought-iron greenhouses replicate exotic climes. The most spectacular of these is the curvy Palm House, built between 1844 and 1848. The Temperate House was the world's largest greenhouse when built in 1899 and contains a Chilean Wine Palm some 18m (60ft) tall and over 150 years old. The Princess of Wales Conservatory is a favourite for its giant water-lily pads, and the exhibition Evolution is a high-tech exploration of the story of the planet to date.

Reminders of the gardens' early royal patronage are provided by tiny Kew Palace (summer home of George III 1802–18), Queen Charlotte's Cottage and the Queen's Garden. Also in the gardens

are notable follies (fanciful buildings), including Kew's distinctive pagoda, plus museums and galleries.
www.kew.org

➕ 140 B3 ✉ Kew, Richmond ☎ 020 8332 5655 🕐 Daily from 9:30. Closes approx 4:15 winter, 6:30 summer. Closed 25 Dec, 1 Jan 👛 Expensive 🍴 Café (£), restaurants (£–££) 🚇 Kew Gardens 🚤 Riverboat to Kew Pier from Westminster and Richmond (Apr–Oct) ❓ Kew Explorer hop-on hop-off land train (moderate). Marine Display in Palm House basement re-creates four marine habitats with fish, corals and other sea creatures

RICHMOND AND TWICKENHAM

These adjoining riverside suburbs make up one of London's most charming and bucolic districts. From Richmond station turn left to walk along George Street. Off here to the right is a lovely village green. Return to George Street and continue to Richmond Bridge and the impressive classical-style riverside development. To visit Richmond Park take bus 371 and get off at the Royal Star & Garter; here you can enjoy the magnificent view down on to the river.

Richmond Park, London's largest royal park and one of its wildest, with herds of deer, is ideal for a picnic. If you want to explore it properly consider renting a bicycle. As an alternative to the park, follow the towpath along the river from Richmond Bridge (it's possible to cycle along here) and after around 30 minutes you will reach **Ham House.** This is an outstanding 17th-century house that has been refurbished to its former glory.

To get to Twickenham (on the opposite side of the river) walk back a short way to the Hammerton Ferry and cross to **Marble Hill House,** a lovely early 1720s Palladian villa. Further on is **Orleans House Gallery,** where art exhibitions are staged in a beautiful baroque octagonal room. To return to Richmond, walk up Orleans Road and catch one of buses that run along the Richmond Road.

➕ 140 B3 ℹ Old Town Hall, Richmond ☎ 020 8940 9125 🕐 Mon–Sat 10–5, also Sun May–Sep only 10:30–1:30

Ham House

✉ Ham Street, Ham ☎ 020 8940 1950;
www.nationaltrust.org.uk ⏰ House: Apr–Oct
Sat–Wed 1–5. Gardens: all year Sat–Wed 11–6
✋ Expensive

Marble Hill House

✉ Richmond Road, Twickenham ☎ 020 8892 5115; www.english-
heritage.org.uk ⏰ Apr–Oct Sat 10–2, Sun and public hols 10–5 ✋ Moderate

Orleans House Gallery

✉ Riverside, Twickenham ☎ 020 8831 6000 ⏰ Tue–Sat 1–5:30, Sun
2–5:30, (4:30 Oct–Mar) ✋ Free

V&A MUSEUM OF CHILDHOOD

The Museum of Childhood started life in 1856 in South Kensington
as a temporary wing of the Victoria and Albert Museum. Its
elaborate, typically Victorian ironwork structure was then moved
wholesale to Bethnal Green and, aside from comfy carpets, new
glass cases and a 1990s café, little has changed since. Reopened
in 2006 after refurbishment, it is still part of the V&A and is a
shrine to childhood and all the accoutrements that go with it, from
birthing stools to children's wartime gas masks, from Javanese
shadow puppets and Steiff teddy bears to Sonic the Hedgehog
and Teletubbies. The museum is as much for adults as for children,
documenting social trends and changes through the medium of
play. Many toys date back centuries and several are exquisite
handmade pieces. The museum is particularly renowned for its
collection of doll's houses. Its doll collection is also comprehensive
and includes some outstanding Japanese ceremonial dolls. There
are children's activities and events workshops, theatre productions
and gallery trails.

www.vam.ac.uk

✚ 140 D2 ✉ Cambridge Heath Road ☎ 020 8983 5200 ⏰ Sat–Thu
10–5:45 ✋ Free; small charge for some activities 🍴 Benugo Café (£)
Ⓔ Bethnal Green ❓ Lovely park next door for picnics

Excursions

BATH

Designated as a UNESCO World Heritage Site, the honey-coloured city of Bath was developed as a fashionable spa in the 18th century and is a perfect example of a Georgian town. It was the **Roman Baths** that first established the city and, still remarkably complete, they form the most impressive Roman remains in Britain. Adjacent is another 'must-see' site, Bath Abbey, dating mostly from the 16th century. A short walk away is the Royal Crescent, built between 1767 and 1774. This glorious terrace of 30 classically inspired three-floor houses in glowing golden Bath stone is often claimed to be the most majestic street in Britain.

Just outside Bath, at Claverton, is the excellent **American Museum,** which features 15 authentically re-created 17th- to 19th-century rooms.

www.visitbath.co.uk

🛈 Abbey Church Yard ☎ 0906 711 2000 (information line; premium rate) 🕒 Mon–Sat 9:30–6 (5 in winter), Sun 10–4

Roman Baths

✉ Stall Street ☎ 01225 477785; www.romanbaths.co.uk 🕒 Jan–Feb, Nov–Dec daily 9:30–5:30; Mar–Jun, Sep–Oct daily 9–6; Jul–Aug daily 9am–10pm (last admission 1 hour before closing) 💷 Expensive

American Museum

✉ Claverton Manor, Bath ☎ 01225 460503; www.americanmuseum.org 🕒 Mid-Mar to Oct Tue–Sun 12–5:30 💷 Moderate

CAMBRIDGE

Cambridge is famous for its university, one of the oldest and most prestigious in Britain, alongside Oxford. The oldest college is Peterhouse, founded in 1284, but the most noted college is King's, established in 1441 and renowned for its magnificent medieval architecture and almost heavenly choir. Outstanding among the other 31 colleges are Queen's, Trinity, Magdalene, St John's, Clare, Jesus and Emmanuel. All the colleges now admit men and women, but Magdalene has done this only since 1988.

The Backs is a strip of grassy meadow-cum-lawns between the rear of the colleges and the River Cam. It is a fine venue for a picnic and is a good place for college-viewing. Spanning the Cam are two famous bridges: the Bridge of Sighs, a copy of the famous Venetian bridge; and the Mathematical Bridge, a wooden crossing now bolted together but originally assembled without a single metal fixing. The town's principal museum is the **Fitzwilliam Museum,** with

outstanding collections of paintings, antiquities, ceramics and armour.
🛈 Wheeler Street ☎ 0871 226 8006 (premium rate); www.visitcambridge.org
🕐 Oct–Mar Mon–Fri 10–5:30, Sat 10–5; Apr–Sep also Sun, bank hol Mon 11–4

Fitzwilliam Museum
✉ Trumpington Street ☎ 01223 332900; www.fitzmuseum.cam.ac.uk 🕐 Tue–Sat 10–5, Sun 12–5. Closed Mon (except Easter Mon and Spring public hol Mon), Good Fri 🎟 Free ❓ Music Sun 1:15

OXFORD

Oxford is synonymous with its university, the oldest in Britain. The most outstanding colleges are Christ Church, New College and Magdalen. Oxford also has plenty of non-university attractions, including the **Ashmolean Museum,** home to one of Britain's finest provincial collections, and the Pitt Rivers Museum, an extraordinary and delightfully old-fashioned Victorian ethnographic treasure-trove. The charming

Covered Market, selling food and clothing plus all sorts of other things, is also worth a visit.
🛈 15–16 Broad Street ☎ 01865 726871 🕐 Mon–Sat 9:30–5, Sun 10–4

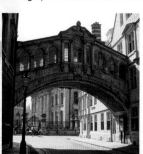

Ashmolean Museum
✉ Beaumont Street ☎ 01865 278000 🕐 Tue–Sat and public hols 10–5, Sun 12–5 🎟 Free

a walk around Oxford

Start from the tourist information centre, where you can pick up maps and leaflets.

At the end of Broad Street, turn left into Cornmarket Street, which leads into St Aldate's Street, and enter Christ Church college through the War Memorial Garden. Exit left from the gate by the Picture Gallery into Oriel Square, named after the college on the right-hand side. Visit the college grounds then continue up Oriel Street to High Street, where you emerge opposite the portico of the University Church of St Mary the Virgin. Visit the church, then leave from the rear entrance into Radcliffe Square.

On your left is Brasenose College, while in the middle of the square is the Radcliffe Camera, built in 1749 and now part of the **Bodleian Library.** Join a tour to see the magnificent Duke Humfrey's Library and Divinity School, a masterpiece of Gothic architecture.

Go through Schools Quad and turn left at the far end.

The domed **Sheldonian Theatre,** ahead, was designed by Sir Christopher Wren between 1663 and 1669. Climb to the top for a view of Oxford's 'dreaming spires'.

Leave the Sheldonian and turn right to reach Catte Street. Pass beneath Oxford's very own Bridge of Sighs, which spans New College Lane.

For a pub lunch turn immediately left into St Helen's Passage and follow it to the famous Turf Tavern.

Return to New College Lane and follow this around to New College, noting the splendid gargoyles and grotesques on the wall. Leaving New College, Queen's Lane takes you between Queen's College (right) and St Edmund Hall (also a college, left).

Turn left into the High Street and walk a little further to Magdalen College (pronounced 'Mordlin'), with luck in time to attend the famous Evensong performance (generally at 6pm, but check with the tourist information centre).

Distance Approx 5km (3 miles)
Time 4–6 hours depending on which colleges are open
Start point Tourist information centre
End point Magdalen College
Lunch Turf Tavern (£) ✉ 4 Bath Place, via St Helen's Passage

Bodleian Library ✉ Broad Street ☎ 01865 277224 🕑 Guided tours all year Mon–Sat 10:30, 11:30, 2, 3 ♿ Moderate

Sheldonian Theatre ✉ Broad Street ☎ 01865 277299 🕑 Mon–Sat 10–12:30, 2–4:30 (3:30 in winter). All times subject to functions ♿ Inexpensive ❓ To find out which colleges are open visit www.ox.ac.uk and follow the Visitors link

WINDSOR

Windsor is famous above all for its spectacularly sited **castle,** which (like the Tower of London) dates back to the time of William the Conqueror and has been continuously occupied since the 11th century. It has been enlarged and remodelled many times, though it took on its basic present shape in the 12th and 14th centuries. The castle is one of the three official residences of the Sovereign (the others are Buckingham Palace and Holyrood House, Edinburgh) and as such is in regular working use. In 1992 it suffered significant fire damage, but all areas have since been fully repaired and restored.

The most impressive of all the castle buildings is St George's Chapel, a masterpiece of English Gothic architecture, completed in 1511. Ten monarchs lie here, including Henry VIII and Charles I. The state apartments are hung with works from the Royal Collection, though the most startling exhibit is Queen Mary's Doll's House. Made in 1921 for the consort to King George V, it was designed in meticulous detail at one-twelfth life-size with working plumbing and elevators, and miniature paintings and books donated by eminent writers and artists of the day.

Windsor town is a busy shopping centre but you can escape the crowds by exploring Windsor Park, perfect for a picnic. Close by, Legoland makes a great day out for young children.

🛈 The Old Booking Hall, Central Station ☎ 01753 743900 🕓 Mon–Fri, Sun 10–4, Sat 10–5. Extended hours in summer

Windsor Castle

✉ Entrance on Castle Hill ☎ 020 7766 7304; 24-hour recorded information 01753 831118 🕓 Daily Mar–Oct 9:45–5:15; Nov–Feb 9:45–4:15. St George's Chapel open Mon–Sat; services only on Sun. Castle/apartments are occasionally closed; reduced admission on these days ✋ Very expensive

Index

Acknowledgements

The Automobile Association wishes to thank the following photographers for their assistance in the preparation of this book.

Abbreviations for the picture credits are as follows – (t) top; (b) bottom; (l) left; (r) right; (c) centre; (AA) AA World Travel Library

4cl Oxford Circus, AA/M Jourdan; **4cc** Interior, St Paul's Cathedral, AA/R Strange; **4cr** Covent Garden, AA/M Jourdan; **5l** Pulteney Bridge, Bath, AA/C Jones; **5c** The London Eye and River Thames, AA/C Sawyer; **5r** Greenwich Park, AA/N Setchfield; **6-7** Oxford Circus, AA/M Jourdan; **10** Parade, Buckingham Palace, AA/M Jourdan; **12** Eurostar train, AA/W Voysey; **13** Canary Wharf station, AA/M Jourdan; **14** London taxi, AA/M Jourdan; **15** Regent's Street, AA/J Tims; **17** Telephone box, AA/S McBride; **20–21** Interior, St Paul's Cathedral, AA/R Strange; **22t** Sculpture outside the British Museum, AA/M Jourdan; **22c** Sculpture from the Elgin Marbles collection, AA; **23t** Queen Elizabeth II Great Court, AA/N Setchfield; **23c** The Nereid Monument, AA/M Trelawny; **24** Street performer, AA/S McBride; **25–26c** Covent Garden, AA/M Jourdan; **25tr** Street entertainer, AA/M Jourdan; **26c** Big Ben, AA/R Victor; **26b** Big Ben and the Houses of Parliament, AA/T Cohen; **27t** Statue of Richard the Lionheart, AA/W Voysey; **28b** Interior, National Gallery, AA/J Tims; **28–29t** Exterior, National Gallery, AA/W Voysey; **30t** Exterior, Natural History Museum, AA/T Woodcock; **30c** Interior, Natural History Museum, AA/M Jourdan; **31** Dinosaur skeleton, Natural History Museum, AA/N Setchfield; **32** St Paul's Cathedral, AA/R Victor; **33t** Cupola, St Paul's Cathedral, AA/B Smith; **33b** Interior, St Paul's Cathedral, AA/T Woodcock; **34** Science Museum, AA/G Wrona; **35** Interior, Science Museum, AA/N Setchfield; **36t** Traitor's Gate, Tower of London, AA/W Voysey; **36–37b** Tower of London, AA/W Voysey; **37t** Beefeater, AA/W Voysey; **38b** The Victoria and Albert Museum, AA/W Voysey; **38–39c** The Victoria and Albert Museum, AA/N Setchfield; **40b** Westminster Abbey, AA/W Voysey; **40–41c** Interior, Westminster Abbey, AA/J Tims; **42–43** Street performer, Covent Garden, AA/M Jourdan; **45** Fountain, Trafalgar Square, AA/M Jourdan; **46t** 'The Apotheosis of James I', Rubens, Banqueting House, AA/J Tims; **46c** Bust of Charles I, Banqueting House, AA/J Tims; **47** Buckingham Palace, London, AA/S McBride; **48** Bandsmen, AA/M Jourdan; **49cr** Churchill's bedroom, AA/M Trelawny; **49b** Jermyn Street, AA/P Kenward; **50** Interior, National Portrait Gallery, AA/J Tims; **51** Piccadilly Circus, AA/J Tims; **52t** Royal Academy of Arts, AA/M Jourdan; **52b** St James Church Market, AA/R Turpin; **53** St James's Palace, AA/W Voysey; **54t** St James's Park, London, AA/R Turpin; **54b** Tobacconists, St James's Street, AA/P Kenward; **55** Spencer House, AA/P Kenward; **56** Fountain by Sir Edwin Lutyens, Trafalgar Square, AA/M Jourdan; **57l** Admiral Lord Nelson, Trafalgar Square AA/W Voysey; **57t** Horse Guards, Whitehall, AA/J McMillan; **58** St Katherine's Dock, AA/P Kenward; **59** Fleet Street, AA/R Mort; **60** Bank of England building, AA/P Kenward; **61t** Courtauld Gallery, AA/J Tims; **62c** Charles Dickens House, AA/R Victor; **62t** Canary Wharf, AA/N Setchfield; **63t** Fleet Street and St Brides, AA/R Mort; **63b** Interior, Guildhall, AA/T Woodcock; **64t** Middle Temple Hall, AA/M Trelawny; **64b** The Monument, AA/J Tims; **65** Lloyd's of London, AA/R Mort; **66** Interior, Temple Church, AA; **67t** Lincoln's Inn, AA/M Trelawny; **68** Lord Mayor State Coach, Museum of London, AA/T Woodcock; **70** Interior, St Bride's Church, AA/M Trelawny; **70–71b** St Katherine Dock, AA/P Kenward; **71r** St Stephen Walbrook, AA/P Kenward; **72t** Sir John Soane's Museum, AA/J Tims; **73b** Tower Bridge, AA/R Victor; **74** Houses of Parliament, AA/B Smith; **75** Tate Modern cafe, AA/M Jourdan; **76** Britain at War Museum, AA/W Voysey; **77** Design Museum, AA/N Setchfield; **78** HMS Belfast, AA/P Kenward; **78–79** Imperial War Museum, AA/B Smith; **80t** Jewel Tower, AA/T Woodcock; **80–81b** London Aquarium, AA/R Turpin; **81t** London Dungeon, AA/N Setchfield; **82** London Eye, AA/M Jourdan; **83** Oxo Tower, AA/N Setchfield; **84t** Globe Theatre, AA/R Turpin; **84b** Globe Theatre, AA/R Turpin; **85t** Crest, Southwark Cathedral, AA/R Turpin; **85b** Southwark Cathedral, AA/R Turpin; **86** Tate Britain, AA/T Woodcock; **87** Tate Modern, AA/M Jourdan; **88t** Westminster Cathedral, AA/R Turpin; **88b** Westminster Cathedral, AA/T Woodcock; **89** Townhouse, Bywater Street, AA/N Setchfield; **90** Apsley House, AA/S & O Matthews; **90b** Cheyne Walk, Chelsea, AA/R Turpin; **91** Harrods, AA/T Woodcock; **92** Chelsea Pensioners, AA/R Strange; **92–93c** Cheyne Walk, Chelsea, AA/R Turpin; **93r** Sir Thomas More, S&O Mathews; **94t** Serpentine, Hyde Park, AA/N Setchfield; **95t** Gate detail, Kensington Palace, AA/S McBride; **94–95b** Kensington Palace Gardens, AA/M Jourdan; **96** Leighton House, AA/J Tims; **98** Deer, Richmond Park, AA/N Setchfield; **99** Richmond, AA/N Setchfield; **100–101** Royal Observatory, AA/N Setchfield; **102–103b** Old Royal Naval College, AA/N Setchfield; **103t** Detail, Cutty Sark, AA/N Setchfield; **104t** Well Walk, Hampstead, AA/R Mort; **104b** Admirals House, Hampstead, AA/S & O Matthews; **105t** View from Parliament Hill, AA/J Tims; **106t** Hampton Court Palace, AA/R Turpin; **107t** Clock, Hampton Court Palace, AA/D Forss; **107b** Hampton Court Palace, AA/R Turpin; **108t** Highgate Cemetery, AA/M Trelawny; **108–109** Library, Kenwood House, AA/J Tims; **110** Temperate House, Royal Botanic Gardens, AA/N Setchfield; **110–111** Temperate House, Royal Botanic Gardens, AA/N Setchfield; **112** Richmond upon Thames, AA/J Miller; **113** Greenwich Park and Royal Observatory, AA/N Setchfield; **114–115** Pulteney Weir, Bath, AA/C Jones; **116** Roman Baths, Bath, AA/C Jones; **117t** Sally Lunn's Bun shop, Bath AA/C Jones; **118b** The Royal Crescent, Bath, AA/C Jones; **118t** Quadrangle, Trinity College, Cambridge, AA/C Coe; **118–119c** Trinity College, Cambridge, AA/C Coe; **119tl** Punting, River Cam, AA/C Coe; **119cr** Radcliffe Camera, Oxford, AA/C Jones; **119b** Bridge of Sighs, Oxford, AA/C Jones; **120–121t** Library, Brasenose College, Oxford, AA/S Day; **120b** Ceiling, Bodleian Library, Oxford, AA; **121r** Sheldonian Theatre, Oxford, AA/A Lawson; **122** Changing of the Guard, Windsor Castle, AA/W Voysey; **123** River Thames and Windsor Castle, AA/J Tims

Every effort has been made to trace the copyright holders, and we apologise in advance for any unintentional omissions or errors. We would be pleased to apply any corrections in any following edition of this publication.

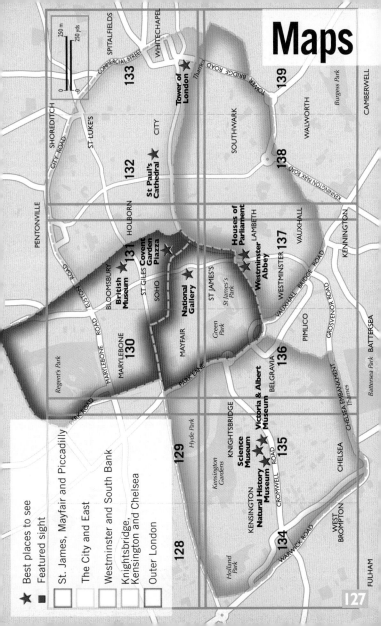

Maps

Best places to see

★ Featured sight

■ St. James, Mayfair and Piccadilly

The City and East

Westminster and South Bank

Knightsbridge, Kensington and Chelsea

Outer London

250 m
250 yds

128
129
130
131
132
133
134
135
136
137
138
139

★ Tower of London

★ St Paul's Cathedral

★ British Museum

★ Covent Garden Piazza

★ National Gallery

★ Houses of Parliament

★ Westminster Abbey

★ Victoria & Albert Museum

★ Science Museum

★ Natural History Museum

SPITALFIELDS
WHITECHAPEL
COMMERCIAL STREET
SHOREDITCH
CITY ROAD
ST. LUKE'S
CITY
SOUTHWARK
WALWORTH
CAMBERWELL
Burgess Park
TOWER BRIDGE ROAD
KENNINGTON PARK ROAD
Thames
PENTONVILLE
HOLBORN
ST GILES
BLOOMSBURY
EUSTON ROAD
MARYLEBONE ROAD
MARYLEBONE
Regent's Park
SOHO
MAYFAIR
PARK LANE
ST JAMES'S
St James's Park
Green Park
WESTMINSTER
LAMBETH
VAUXHALL
VAUXHALL BRIDGE ROAD
PIMLICO
BELGRAVIA
GROSVENOR ROAD
CHELSEA EMBANKMENT
Battersea Park
BATTERSEA
KENNINGTON
PARK ROAD
KNIGHTSBRIDGE
Hyde Park
Kensington Gardens
KENSINGTON
CROMWELL ROAD
WARWICK ROAD
WEST BROMPTON
FULHAM
CHELSEA
Holland Park

127

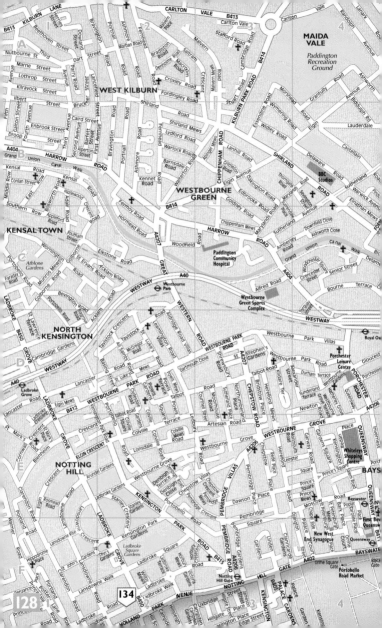

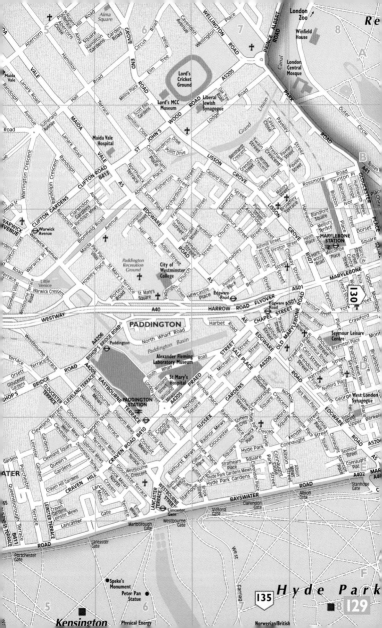

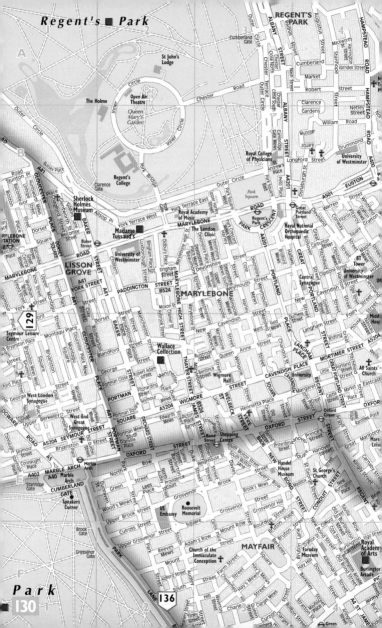

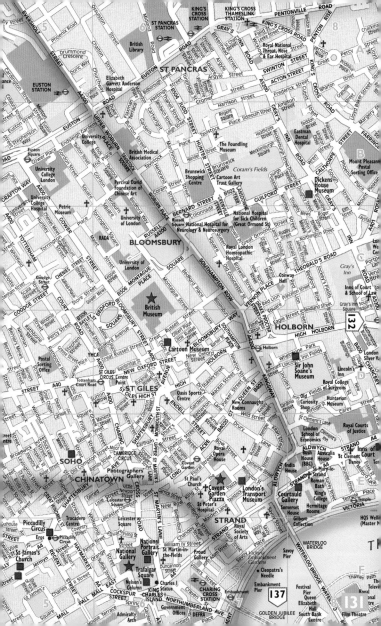

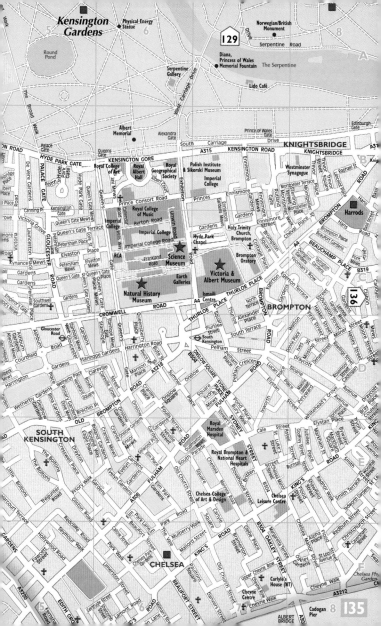

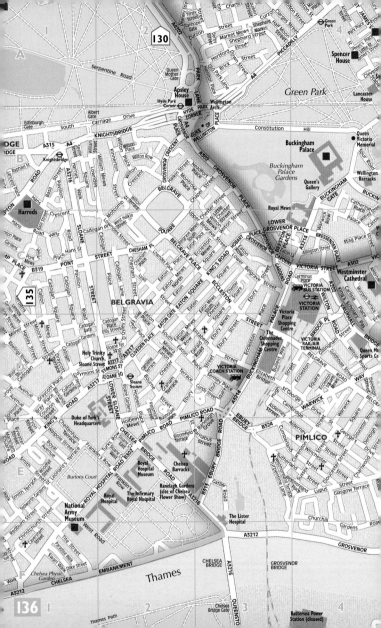

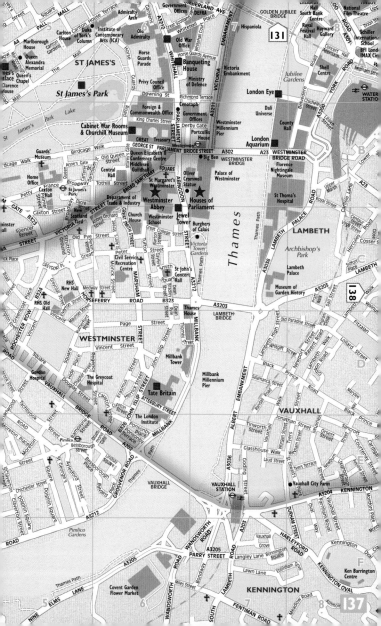

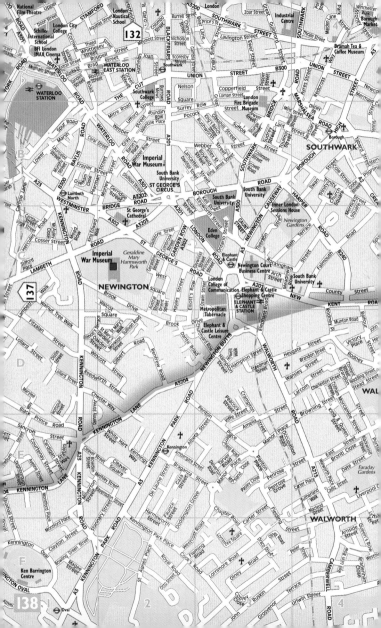

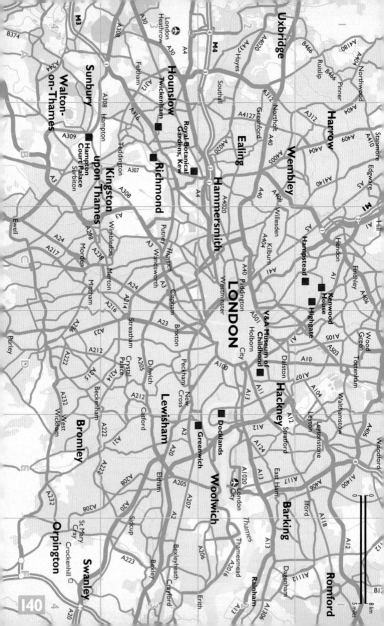

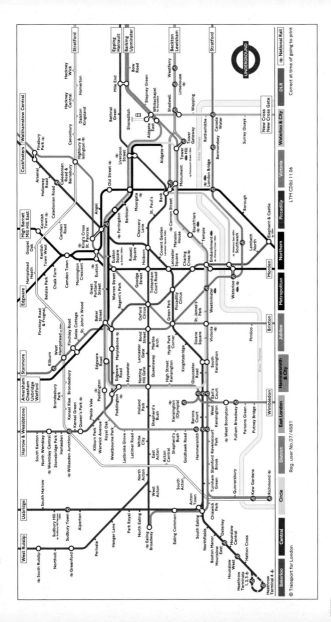

UNDERGROUND

© Transport for London

LTM CD(b) 11.06

Correct at time of going to print

Reg. user No.07/4681

Bakerloo   Central   Circle   District   East London   Hammersmith & City   Jubilee   Metropolitan   Northern   Piccadilly   Victoria   Waterloo & City   DLR ⇌   National Rail ⇌

141

Notes

Notes

Notes